Anita Anand is a development and mutlimedia communications specialist, writer and water colour artist.

She began her forty-plus years career in developing science teaching programmes for rural school children in Madhya Pradesh. She has worked as a policy analyst in Washington DC, and was Director of the Women's Feature Service, an international service of development writing by women journalists, in Italy and later in India. She has been travelling to Afghanistan since 2004, working with UN agencies and international and national civil society organisations.

She is the author of *The Beauty Game* and co-editor of *World Social Forum: Challenging Empires* and *Whose World is it Anyway? The United Nations, Civil Society and the Multilateral Future.*

Kabul Blogs

my days in the life of Afghanistan

ANITA ANAND

sketches and illustrations by the author

women
UNLIMITED
an associate of
kali for women

Kabul Blogs: my days in the life of Afghanistan
was first published in India in 2016
by
Women Unlimited
(an associate of Kali for Women)
7/10, FF, Sarvapriya Vihar
New Delhi – 110016

www.womenunlimited.net

ISBN: 978-8188965-84-7

Cover design: Neelima Rao

Printed at Raj Press, R-3, Inderpuri, New Delhi – 110012

Kabul

Ah! How beautiful is Kabul encircled by her arid mountains
And Rose, of the trails of thorns she envies
Her gusts of powdered soil slightly sting my eyes
But I love her, for knowing and loving are born of this same
dust
My song exalts her dazzling tulips
And at the beauty of her trees, I blush
How sparkling the water flows from Pul-i-Mastaan!
May Allah protect such beauty from the evil eye of man!
Khizr chose the path to Kabul in order to reach Paradise
For her mountains brought him close to the delights of heaven
From the fort with sprawling walls a dragon of protection
Each stone there is more precious than the treasure of Shayagan
Every street of Kabul is enthralling to the eye
Through the bazaars, caravans of Egypt pass
One could not count the moons that shimmer on her roofs
And the thousand splendid suns that hide behind her walls

— *Saib-e-Tabrizi, 17th century poet*

Afghanistan: Provinces

Source: Central Statistics Office

The boundaries and names shown on this map do not imply official endorsement or acceptance by the United Nations or Relief Web. These maps may be freely distributed. If more current information is available, please update the maps and return them to Relief Web for posting.

Preface

This book is based on the blog called *Letter from Afghanistan* that I started writing during my second visit to Afghanistan in 2006, to share my experiences in and of the country.

My first trip to Afghanistan in 2004 was also my first to any 'post-conflict' country. Though not very long, the visit got me excited about the journey of Afghanistan as it recovered from decades of instability and violence. While there, I personally did not experience any threat to my life, and met many generous Afghans and heard their stories of exile, bombings, life under the Taliban and their hopes for a new and modern Afghanistan. The air, full of anticipation of better times, was infectious.

Back in India, I could not stop thinking about Afghanistan. I followed the news media religiously, but all I found were stories of insurgency and violence and nothing that described the Afghanistan I had experienced. As a development and communications professional, I know that mainstream media focus on bad news, with journalists trained to segregate stories into 'soft' and 'hard' news. While these lines have blurred in recent times, preference is still given to politics, economics and wars—fought, won and lost. The same was true of news emanating from Afghanistan. How then were people to know and understand the varied nature of joys and sorrows of everyday Afghanistan?

The little I knew about Afghanistan came from my experience of visiting and working in the country, supplemented by media reports, and fiction and non-fiction written by Afghans raised outside the country but who had knowledge, insight and great love for their culture and people. Then there were the books written by foreign correspondents or diplomats posted in Afghanistan, and popular commercial and documentary films.

I have made multiple trips to Afghanistan on different assignments since 2006, and have developed long-standing friendships with Afghans and expats who have worked or continue to work in Afghanistan. What binds us is our common experience of and love for Afghanistan.

The nature of my assignments and the precarious security situation have meant that I have not travelled much in the country, and therefore cannot pretend to have great exposure to the many kinds of Afghanistans that exist, side by side. I do not possess a nuanced understanding of the rich history and traditions of Afghanistan; I also do not speak Dari and Pashto, or the other languages spoken in the country fluently, so as to have deep conversations with the local people who are most comfortable in their native languages. However, I am a keen observer of people—their history, what makes them the way they are, what motivates them and how they see themselves and the world around them.

This book is not meant to provide a comprehensive account of life in Afghanistan; it is not an investigative report or a scholarly work. It is a deeply personal view of my time in Afghanistan, my limited experiences and the people and situations I encountered. While writing it some of the feedback I received was about the blogs not reflecting the persistent political activity and violence in Afghanistan. It is not that I was not aware of the violence in Afghanistan, but my desire here was to provide representation to the Afghanistan that I had experienced. I believe that in writing about what I saw, what moved me, what I related to and what I loved about

Afghanistan, I am writing about how Afghanistan changed in front of my eyes and how it changed me in the process.

The author Chinua Achebe says, among other things, about his writing:

> I do not think the world needs to be told stories of despair; there is enough despair as it is without anyone adding to it. If we have any role at all, I think it is the role of optimism, not blind or stupid optimism, but the kind which is meaningful, one that is rather close to that notion of the world which is not perfect, but which can be improved. In other words, we do not just sit and hope that things will work out; we have a role to play to make that come about. That seems to me to be the reason for the existence of the writer.

Achebe's words resonate with me. I take the role of the optimist that Achebe writes about somewhat seriously. I did not want to write about despair. I believe that the world we live in can be improved, and my role is that of one who engages constructively with the world around her.

It is now 2015, Afghanistan has a new government, a new president, a chief executive officer and new cabinet of ministers. There is hope and there is apprehension, both within and outside Afghanistan. The future of the country, that I love dearly besieged by decades of violence and clan driven politics, hangs in a balance.

2004

"Children, everybody, here's what to do during war: In a time of destruction, create something. A poem. A parade. A community. A school. A vow. A moral principle. One peaceful moment."

– Maxine Hong Kingston, *The Fifth Book of Peace*

Afghanistan in 2004

Even before my first visit to Afghanistan in 2004, the country had already been wracked by over two decades of war and civil unrest. The Soviet Union invaded in 1979, but was forced to withdraw ten years later by the anti-communist mujahideen forces. The Communist regime collapsed in 1992. The fighting that erupted among the various mujahideen factions eventually helped to spawn the Taliban, a hard-line, Pakistan-sponsored movement that fought to end the culture of warlords and civil war which gripped the country.

More than a quarter of the population of 28 million was displaced during this period and between one and two million people were killed—around five per cent of the population. Physical and social infrastructure was devastated as Afghanistan sank to the bottom of the Human Development Index.

During the Taliban period (1994–2001), virtual gender apartheid was introduced. Women were banned from working outside the home; they were forced to wear the burqa and had to be escorted by a *muharam* (a male relative). Girls' schools were closed down all over the country. In 2002, only five per cent of women were literate, 54 per cent of girls under the age of 18 were married, and the maternal mortality rate was the second highest in the world, with an estimated 15,000 women dying each year from pregnancy-related causes.[1]

On October 7, 2001, after the Taliban's refusal to expel Osama bin Laden from Afghanistan, the United States led an international coalition of states in a military campaign to oust the Taliban. Called 'Operation Enduring Freedom', the Taliban were defeated and warlord-led opposition groups, including the Northern Alliance, regained control of Kabul. While the effort to disband the Taliban and capture bin Laden continued, the United Nations began working with Afghan expatriates and the Northern Alliance to try and rebuild the country and create a stable governing body.

In the post-Taliban era, the government's capacity was either significantly weakened or rendered completely non-existent in some parts of the country. Due to the long-term sanctions, Afghanistan's economy was in a precarious and fragile state. Key government institutions had no qualified staff and many others had to be more or less built from scratch.

Rebuilding Afghanistan

According to the National Democratic Institute, the demise of the Taliban provided a new opportunity for Afghans to rebuild their country. While the military offensive continued on the ground, the United Nations took the lead in international reconstruction efforts in Afghanistan. Promising to leave a "light footprint" and allowing the Afghan citizens to rebuild their own country, the United Nations brought together the leading Afghan groups to Bonn, Germany, in November 2001, to discuss plans for a future government in Afghanistan.

The groups included the Northern Alliance, which represented the governments driven from power by the Taliban in 1996, under Ahmad Shah Massoud, Abdul Rashid Dostum, and Burhanuddin Rabbani; the Rome Group, which represented the former King Zahir Shah; the Peshawar Group, which represented millions of Afghan refugees in Pakistan; and the Cyprus Group, which represented an Iranian backed group of Afghan exiles.

This meeting in Germany culminated with the signing of the Bonn Agreement, which provided for short-term power-sharing among the groups listed above and established a timetable for a two-year transitional period.

The Bonn agreement stipulated that an interim administration be established to govern Afghanistan for the first six months of 2002. Its immediate function was to facilitate the provision and distribution of internal aid in the country. The interim administration's most important function was to convene a Loya Jirga, a council of tribal leaders, in June 2002. King Zahir Shah, who returned to Afghanistan on April 18, presided over the gathering to give the process legitimacy, but otherwise played a largely ceremonial role. The meeting was unofficially chaired by representatives of the US government and Lakhdar Brahimi, the United Nations' special representative for Afghanistan. The Loya Jirga, in turn, elected a Transitional Authority to govern until a representative government was elected by mid-2004.

Hamid Karzai, a Pashtun who broke with the Taliban early and had a long-standing friendship with the former King, Zahir Shah, was appointed Chairman of the interim administration. Pashtun representation in the government was otherwise relatively low, with a dominant presence of the Northern Alliance, including General Mohammed Fahim, Younis Qanooni, and Abdullah Abdullah, who were ethnic Tajiks from the Panshjeer valley. Pashtuns from the southern regions of Afghanistan—including Kandahar, the Taliban's stronghold—had little representation in the new government.

As stipulated by the Bonn Agreement, on June 9, 2002, the Emergency Loya Jirga was convened. The Loya Jirga brought more than 1,700 Afghans from across the country to Kabul, charged with selecting a broad-based, representative government. The attendees included tribal or regional leaders, political, military and religious figures, royalty, and government officials, etc.

There are no time limits to the Loya Jirga process and it continues until there is a decision reached by consensus, with no formal votes taken. The mixed results of Afghanistan's Emergency Loya Jirga were largely a result of conditions in which it was held. As the international peacekeeping forces were not extended beyond Kabul so as to neutralize regional warlords, the politics of intimidation affected the election of delegates and influenced the major decisions at the Loya Jirga. Afghans had gathered at the Loya Jirga to help shape their new government but, according to some participants, the process lacked democratic legitimacy with decisions being taken arbitrarily and in a top-down fashion. Allegations that the process was being controlled "from behind the scenes" by the international community also plagued the Emergency session.

On June 19, 2002, Hamid Karzai was officially sworn in by the Loya Jirga as the President of Afghanistan. Ten days later, Karzai appointed a cabinet to lead the newly established Afghan Transitional Administration (ATA). Many of the warlords and tribal leaders successfully manoeuvred the decision-making process to secure cabinet posts and almost all high level positions for themselves, as only two civilians with non-military histories were made ministers.

Under the Bonn Agreement, the ATA was responsible for drafting and implementing a new constitution. The constitutional drafting process was viewed by many political analysts and observers to be problematic, as a number of electoral issues that would be covered in the new constitution—the type of electoral system to govern the country, the role of political parties in the electoral system, and the role of women and minorities in the new government, for example—were designed to be addressed in a public consultative process before the final document would be ratified, but this process was limited by the government's refusal to release its draft of the constitution at the time of the consultations, thus preventing citizens from commenting on the actual document.

A Constitutional Loya Jirga (CLJ) was convened in mid-December 2003 which, after three weeks of deliberation, ratified Afghanistan's new constitution on January 4, 2004. The CLJ comprised of 450 elected delegates, including reserved seats for women, minorities and refugees, and 52 delegates appointed by President Karzai, half of whom were women. Many observers reported intimidation and vote buying throughout the election process, enabling warlords and Islamists to make a strong showing at the Jirga. The new constitution called for a strong presidential system of government, but gave the national assembly—which would consist of the Wolesi Jirga (House of People) and a Meshrano Jirga (House of Elders)—oversight powers, including the right to impeach ministers and approve cabinet appointments.

The constitution also stipulated that men and women have equal rights and duties before the law. Although Sharia law was not mentioned explicitly in the constitution, it established Afghanistan as an Islamic republic with Islam as its "sacred religion," mandating that "no law shall contravene the tenets and provisions of the holy religion of Islam in Afghanistan".[2]

Two other controversial issues settled in the Jirga were the anointment of the former King Mohammad Zahir Shah as the "Father of the Nation" for his lifetime, and Pashto and Dari being recognised as the national languages, with other minority languages made official languages in the areas where they were spoken.

Though the constitution stated that "every effort will be

made" to hold the presidential and parliamentary elections at the same time, slow progress on improving the security situation and registering voters prompted the transitional government to announce that the presidential and parliamentary elections would take place separately; the presidential election was held in October 2004, while the parliamentary and provincial council elections were scheduled for September 2005.

Financing Afghanistan

Afghanistan received a great deal of attention in the initial years following the fall of the Taliban regime, which resulted in international aid pouring in. In January 2002 at the International Conference on Reconstruction Assistance to Afghanistan held in Tokyo, a cumulative sum of US $4.5 billion was pledged in financial aid by 61 countries and 21 international organisations to be spread over a period of five years. By April 2002, a National Development Framework was prepared that formed the "conceptual basis for the development budget, where the programs will be costed, hard choices made, and specific projects presented".

Two years later, in April 2004, at the International Afghanistan Conference in Berlin, a multi-year commitment of US $8.2 billion was made for the reconstruction and development of Afghanistan for the fiscal years March 2004–March 2007. This commitment was to ensure that Afghanistan's governance and security institutions were reconstructed, development goals met, and poverty alleviation ensured.

However, there continued to be concerns about the security situation and its impact on the development goals. The

International Crisis Committee reported that the international community's failure to extend a strong security umbrella beyond Kabul was perpetuating and indeed deepening the political and economic power of regional commanders.

On March 9, 2004, as I sat in Kabul, the UN Commission on the Status of Women at its 48th session received a draft text on the "situation of women and girls in Afghanistan". It urged that the Afghan Transitional Administration and future governments ensure that the legislative, administrative and other measures support the full enjoyment by women and girls of human rights and fundamental freedoms, including by mainstreaming gender issues into its activities, and to fully implement the Convention on the Elimination of All Forms of Discrimination against Women. It urged the authorities to strengthen efforts to prevent and eliminate violence against women by using legislative measures, and to bring to justice those responsible for violence against women and girls.

March 2004: The first visit

In November 2003, I was asked by a UN agency if I would like to conduct a mid-term evaluation of their Media and Gender Project in Afghanistan. Having not had any kind of links or even sufficient knowledge about the country, needless to say, I was surprised, but said yes. It was decided that I would leave in December 2003, but the trip was indefinitely postponed due to security reasons, and it was only in mid-February of 2004 that I was suddenly asked to leave in ten days' time. With my travel arrangements sorted, I spent the remaining time trying to familiarise myself with the project at hand. I read the background documents provided by the UN agency and searched online for information on gender and media in Afghanistan. Though the material online was not of much help, I had just enough to build a picture in my mind.

My air ticket was routed through Dubai because, as a UN consultant, I could only travel in a United Nations Humanitarian Air Service (UNHAS) flight—an inter-agency air passenger and cargo service for humanitarian and development institutions and their NGO partners in Afghanistan.

I took a private carrier from Delhi to Dubai, spent the night at an airport hotel and boarded the UNHAS flight to Kabul the next morning. This relatively short flight was my first personal experience of the varied landscape and culture of the country. From snow-covered peaks set against clear blue skies that I saw through my plane window, I landed to fighter planes on the tarmac and a sea of brown.

The airport was a modest building, with four immigration lines made up of Afghans and some expats. I cleared immigration and noticed how the officers lingered just a little bit longer over the passport of the very attractive woman in front of me in the queue. After clearing Customs, I was met by Masooda, the woman who would work with me on the project for the next ten days. Masooda and I drove out of the airport through roads with weathered cars, buses and delivery vans.

We passed many men and women bundled up to help them fight the chill in the air, and cyclists pedalling along gracefully on the sides of the road. Most buildings looked recently completed, and the older ones were riddled with bullets or were partly in ruin. The men on the sidewalks wore the traditional salwar kameeze, with the woollen *pakol* headgear and shawls. Some women were wearing sky blue burqas that covered them from head to toe. The shops were modest with their products, and something about being there at that moment made me reminisce about India of the late 1950s.

At the guest house I was told that there was no booking in my name and was directed to another guest house on Flower Street. It was smaller and cosier. Besides, I quite liked the idea of being on a street named Flower!

As Afghanistan is a non-family station, everyone, in a sense, is single. Expats are lodged in 'guest houses' in a communal setting which reminded me of my shared housing during college in the US. My housemates in college were American women; in Kabul, it was a mixture of men and women from France, Nepal, India and Japan, all working as short-term or long-term consultants.

The next day I met the staff who managed the project I was to evaluate and was given a roster of people I needed to interview. The UN agency office was in the United Nations Development Programme (UNDP) compound that had a heavily guarded entrance. Not only was the UN car that I was in searched, but I also had to hold up and produce my pass for the guards to verify. The staff worked in concrete buildings and prefabricated structures that had a large garden with flowers in the central area. The roses were in bloom and yellow jasmine creepers covered the sides of the compound buildings.

At a security briefing, I learned what I could or could not do during my stay in Kabul. I was not allowed to walk on the streets alone, could only travel in a UN vehicle that picked me up in the morning and dropped me off at the end of the day. I could only eat at restaurants that were cleared by security and report every evening at 7:00 p.m. through a walkie-talkie. This was all very new to me. Though taken aback by the level of security, I was not afraid.

Those ten days went in a flash as I met people at the UN and donor agencies funding media projects, NGOs who handled the projects and offered journalistic training, people at the Ministry of Information and Culture (MOIC) and the Ministry of Women's Affairs (MOWA), journalists and media managers, and women who owned and edited women's magazines.

There was a sense of excitement in the air, as if everyone was part of a bigger project to build something new. There was much hope but there was also pessimism. I experienced a country and people that had been destroyed—in almost all aspects of life. While visiting a journalism professor at Kabul University, I saw the work of the Taliban: the library resembled a ghost town with burnt and hacked chairs and tables and broken cabinet glasses. The professor, with a faraway look in his watery eyes, said "it is all finished". Almost all the Afghans I met had a story about loss of loved ones and homes, of migration and return, of sadness and hope. But this experience did not seem to have made them angry or bitter. Just sad.

On March 8, International Women's Day, I attended a function where President Karzai was speaking on the role of women in rebuilding Afghanistan. Striking in his *chapan* and *karakul* hat, he delivered a mesmerising, charismatic and passionate speech on the future of Afghanistan and the role of women. I didn't understand any Dari, but I could sense the essence of his speech. I felt that he was speaking to me to tell me that I also had a role in the making of a new Afghanistan!

Despite the security warning, I felt safe as I walked down Flower Street by myself. As its name suggests, it was once the street to go to for the freshest tulips and roses, but now all I could find were artificial flowers, which also ubiquitously adorned the offices of the bureaucrats I visited. On the first day, I stood hesitantly outside a mini department store, as it was called, and wondered if I should go in. "Salaam," said a well built, tall man, who had the presence of an owner, as he invited me to come in. He asked me where I was from, and smiled and ushered me in when I said I was an Indian. We introduced ourselves and he told me his name was Abdul.

"Tea?" he asked. Yes, if it is not a problem. "How can tea be a problem?" he said, with a broad smile. Soon there was fresh naan, cheese and honey.

We talked, exchanging pleasantries, and when his phone rang, I walked around the store, looking at shelves full of canned goods from the US, Pakistan, Iran and India. There were biscuits, tea bags, coffee—instant and filter—pre-cooked food items and cans of vegetables, cheeses, butter, honey, condensed and dry milk.

Abdul was as keen to know about my life in Delhi as I was about his in Kabul. From that day onwards, he offered me, every morning at 7:00 a.m. without fail, a cup of *sabz* (green) tea, fresh naan, cheese, honey and walnuts. And this chance encounter led to Abdul becoming my first Afghan friend and contact, outside of my work.

As an Indian, I was greeted by many Afghans on the streets as Indian movies and film music have endeared us to the Afghans. Many sought refuge across the border in Pakistan and India and knew Urdu, and there are DVDs of Hindi movies in many stores.

Almost every Afghan I talked to had been affected by the decades of war and violence in the country. Masooda told me how all the men in her family—father, brothers and brothers-in-law—were killed by the Taliban. After 2001, she returned to Kabul with her ailing mother, a younger sister and a school going brother.

Friday is also Jumma, and the prayers are followed by a

sermon by the Imams focusing on current topics of interest. In the afternoons, they visit family, go to parks and gardens and generally relax.

At the Flower Street guesthouse, I came to know a little bit about the other residents. There was a French Food and Agriculture Organisation (FAO) representative who always ate after everyone had finished dinner, by himself. He had one piece of meat with a vegetable lightly cooked, a green salad and a glass of wine. One day he asked me to have a glass of wine with him. We chatted about various things including Italy, where he was posted at the FAO headquarters, and I had also worked earlier at a third world news agency.

There was no dinner at the guest house on Friday as the cook had a day off due to Jumma. I offered to cook an Indian dinner and made chicken curry, dhal, cauliflower, yogurt raita with pomegranates, rice and pooris. The Nepali housemate volunteered to help with the pooris. As we fried the pooris over the hot oil, he told me about his wife and her fine cooking, and the Frenchman brought out several bottles of wine. It was a great evening. After the meal some of us gathered around the TV and watched a DVD of the Indian ghazal singer, Jagjit Singh, in concert, brought by the Nepali housemate.

A week into my stay in Kabul, on my walk down Flower Street, I stepped into a shop three doors down from the guest house. I walked past it every day on my morning walk-and-tea schedule with Abdul. The owner, an old man in a salwar kameeze and cap, propped against the worn out green wooden shutter with a cigarette in his hands, would smile and greet me.

Walking up the staircase, I entered what seemed to be like Aladdin's cave—kilims, gems, crystals, clothes and other Afghan antiquities. He offered tea as I sat on the floor to have a chat. He showed me the lapis lazuli—a crystal prized since ancient times for its intense blue colour. It was found in the Badakhshan province in north-eastern Afghanistan, where the Sar-e-Sang mine deposits have existed for more than 6,000 years. In ancient times, lapis lazuli was known as sapphire, which is the name that is used today for the blue corundum variety. It has also been used in the Taj Mahal in India and can be found in abundance in Afghanistan.

The old man showed me the single ruby that sat on its white calcite/dolomite marble, dotted with hexagonal hooks of muscovite, something I had never seen before and one that amazed me by its sheer beauty. He then took out the kilims. Although I do not know much about them I have always been attracted to them. I was frank with the old man and asked him to show me what he considered to be best-suited for me. I looked through what he had selected and chose a few. He smiled to signal his approval and I asked him to keep my selection aside as I would come to collect them the day before I left.

Adjacent to the Flower Street is the Chicken Street. Once upon a time it was a chicken market, but not anymore. Now the chicken shops have been replaced by stores selling antiques and local craft items. I found some traditional headgear for men, black and red hand-embroidered shawls for gifts and some kilims, of course.

With the collection from the stores in Flower and Chicken Streets, I lobbied for a larger room with an attached bathroom which had just been vacated on the ground floor of the guest house. It led into the garden and there was more natural light coming in. As I arranged my purchases on the available surfaces and the kilims on the floor, the room started to feel

An Uzbeki kilim

like home. At night, as I fell asleep, the light from the gas heater cast an orange glow over the room and my purchases. It was a perfect lullaby.

Soon it was time to leave but I felt that I could have stayed longer. I was fascinated by what I saw and heard. The people were very kind and generous and the expats I met at work were here to participate in the process of rebuilding Afghanistan. As I was leaving Kabul, with a plethora of images and experiences, I felt excited about the possibilities and the future of a new Afghanistan.

2006

History is the third parent.

– Nadeem Aslam, *The Blind Man's Garden*

March 2006: Back in Kabul

Two years to the date and I was back in Kabul for a three-month assignment to train Afghan journalists.

Before leaving India, family and friends expressed concern about my safety in Afghanistan and the long duration of my trip. In 2004, I was not aware of the security situation there but assumed that if the UN had people in Afghanistan, it must be safe. This time around, however, I did know.

I was very excited about this opportunity. Training journalists in a developing country was very close to my heart. Having spent 15 years working with journalists around the world and then four years away from it, I had to say yes. Besides, I was keen to be in Afghanistan again.

It was winter and I was asked to carry sturdy footwear (to negotiate the mud and slush after the snows melt), sunglasses (to shield my eyes from the harsh sun), decent clothing (no unnecessary skin exposure) and whatever prescription medicines I needed.

As in 2004, I stayed in a group house in the Karte seh area of Kabul, south of the centre, on Darulaman road, leading out of the city. It was a lovely large property with a huge, mostly wild garden. There was what I called the glass room, with floor to ceiling glass windows on three sides, rose creepers hugging some part of the glass, and a view of the garden.

My room was on the first floor, leading onto the terrace, with spectacular views of the setting sun in the west. It took me about a week to get completely set-up for my work. There were multiple windows on an entire wall of the room, covered with heavy synthetic velvet maroon curtains, keeping out the lovely winter light. I decided to replace them and took the help of Miriam, a colleague, and Aziz, our designated driver, to take

Karte seh house

me to the open market by the Kabul River where I bought white voile with a small calico print for curtains. Faiz, the caretaker, measured the windows, bought spring curtain holders, and Fatima, the house cleaner, sewed the curtains for me.

On the floor was wall-to-wall grey carpeting. After vacuuming it hard, I decided it needed some brightening up and so I took a trip to Chicken Street and found three kilims. As we worked on the curtains, Faiz told me that the guest house used to be an office earlier and the surplus furniture was kept in one room. We immediately raided the room and found two bookcases and brought them back to my room. I created a makeshift personal area—with a hand mirror, my cosmetics and jewellery. There was a single bed with a two-section side table. I salvaged a table lamp from the store room, and put it next to the bed.

Desks, I needed desks. I got two writing desks from the store room; one became a work desk with my laptop, speakers, some cards and books. A deep blue Herati glass became a holder for my pens and pencils and I situated this desk near the bokhari which was fuelled by coal every evening.

I put the other desk under a window that looked out to the mountains. On this, I placed a locally made basket and some artefacts from Istalif, a mountain town which houses a colony of potters. Looking out of the window, as I was doing my yoga, I could see the mountains behind the house next door. Faiz told me that it was being torn down, and so I quickly did a water colour of it.

I loved my room. The light coming through the calico curtains was divine, especially on moonlit nights, and I had enough space to stretch and do yoga. My housemate, Aleksandr, acquired a set of speakers for me from the guest house store room and I enjoyed listening to my music on the computer. I felt happy working on my table, surrounded by things I had chosen and found.

Aleksandr had also set up the Internet connection. One day, as I was on the computer, I discovered the world of blogging and wrote my first blog: 'Daily life in Kabul'. About a week later, when I went back to the site, I saw people had commented on the blog, asking me for more information about Kabul, Afghanistan, my work, etc. I was delighted and encouraged to write more and gradually learned how to upload photos, with the assistance of a fellow blogger.

I finally settled into a routine. On waking up at around 6:00 or 7:00 a.m., I would go down to the kitchen and make tea—with ginger, cardamom and milk. A little later, I would make breakfast and then get ready for the day.

Fridays and Saturdays were reserved for water colouring,

trips to Chicken Street, and lunch and dinner with friends. Sometimes, there were picnics and day trips out of Kabul. By 10:00 p.m., I was usually in bed. There was very little TV watching, no newspapers, and no chilling out in the city—and I didn't miss any of it.

As I was enjoying my semi-idyllic life, the human security situation in Afghanistan was precarious. The insurgency was intensifying, especially in the southern provinces which were the most volatile in the country and considered to be highly dangerous. Bombings occurred almost daily in these cities and western interests were the usual targets. Banditry and roadside bombs were abundant, and the roads from Kandahar to Kabul and Herat were the most dangerous in the country. The government lacked legitimacy, as it included former warlords and commanders in key positions. Crime and human rights violations were widespread, especially against women, unemployment was high, access to public services was weak, and non-existent in some areas, and poppy cultivation was increasing.

The international community—the United Nations, the Bonn Process community-based reconstruction programmes—had contributed to stabilisation and the establishment of political institutions; but some analysts and critics argued that progress was hampered by an overly top-down approach in which stability took precedence over justice. The scale and inefficiency of the international effort, the absence of a regional approach that would tackle insurgency by dealing with instability in neighbouring countries, stringent security regulations, and an excessive preoccupation with time-frames were some other problems inhibiting the progress made in Afghanistan.

On the positive side, since 2000, when the Taliban had been

overthrown, UN statistics showed that three elections had been held and democratic institutions established formally; some five million refugees had returned to Afghanistan and about four million girls were back in school.

The September 2005 parliamentary and provincial elections were the first in more than 30 years, and in December of the same year, the new parliament held its inaugural session. In February 2006, at the international donors meeting in London, more than US $10 billion was pledged as reconstruction aid over five years.

Day by day in Kabul

While local and international news media focused on the insecurity and violence in the country, life went on as usual for most people in Kabul.

From the bakers who produced the delicious naan, shaped like a very large flattened egg or a flat circular crater with pits, to the vendors selling chewing gum and scratch cards for mobile phones, to beggars and street workers—it was all in a day's work. Men and women go to work, children go to school, and the sun rises and sets every day.

Kabul is at its best at night. The lights twinkle in the mountainside houses and the darkness camouflages the brown of the city. There are only a few cars to be seen and the buses also stop plying on the roads.

Day or night, Kabul is a quiet city. One hardly hears horns, music or loud voices. Breaking this silence is the roar of generators, usually diesel driven, that make up for the lack of power in the city. Water, another prized item here, is delivered to the guest house in a tanker.

When the Taliban fled Kabul in 2001 in the face of the post-

Naan shop in Kabul

9/11 US bombing campaign, they left a city wrecked by years of war. Half the city was turned into rubble. It was a city on life-support, with acute shortages of almost everything, including power and water. Even in 2006, for most people in Kabul, electricity and clean water remained a distant aspiration. War, under-investment, lack of technical and management capacity decimated the power sector. This is crucial as power availability is critical to achieving development and reconstruction goals.

To meet serious power shortfalls, the government added 16–20 MW by installing 25 diesel generators, which included 15 generators for Kabul. In addition, the private sector, through diesel generation, provided an estimated 93 MW. In 2006, Kabul's total available power supply, of around 205 MW, fell seriously short of the estimated requirement of 310 MW, necessitating programmed load-shedding and regular outages at severe economic loss.

The water situation was no better. Rugged and landlocked, Afghanistan has had historical disputes with its Central and South Asian neighbours over the flow of water from mountain rivers which are used to irrigate most of its crops. It loses about two-thirds of its water from rain and snow, annually. For centuries, because of its geographical location, most of the water from Afghanistan's main river basins has poured north to central Asia, east to Pakistan or west to Iran.

Pakistan and Iran spent billions of dollars in recent decades building dams and reservoirs to store water for consumption and generating power. Afghanistan has failed to do so because of the three decades of war and has ended up ruining its water infrastructure. This has resulted in only 25 per cent of Afghanistan's estimated 28 million people having access to clean water. With just one per cent of the 23,000 megawatts of hydroelectricity it needs available, the country has less water than needed for growing wheat and other food commodities.

Kabul is rather spread out and some areas are better developed than others. Most streets and houses have no names or numbers, for security reasons. Many Afghan refugees who moved back to their country were placed in makeshift homes on the hillsides. If you took the roads close to the hillsides, you could see women, men and children carrying jerry cans up the hills, and clothes drying in front of their homes.

In the markets and shops, there is a variety of fruits and vegetables, from bright orange keenus (a tangerine like citrus fruit) and apples to a local squash that looks like zucchini, and eggplant. And, of course, there is dry fruit, in large open sacks—pistachios, raisins, walnuts, figs, apricots, and almonds. Being a North Indian, it is the dry fruit that I love.

There are more men than women on the street. Many women wear the head-to-toe characteristic blue burqas, while there are also those who wear long skirts or loose pants, with a long shirt, a jacket, and a headscarf. Most children in the markets are working, trying to sell gum or other small items. They know a smattering of English and trail you down the street and through the market, making it difficult to shake them off.

This week there are many holidays. March 21 is Nawroz, the local New Year, based on a solar calendar. March 22 is Education Day, and Fridays and Saturdays are holidays every week.

For Nawroz, I am told many people go to Mazar-e-Sharif, the sprawling urban centre and relatively modern city bordering Uzbekistan. Here, Nawroz is also known as Gul-e-Surkh after the abundant red tulips that grow wild around the city and are associated with prosperity and fertility. It is also famous for the hidden tomb of Ali, Prophet Mohammed's son-in-law, buried in a local village. This shrine is the focus of the national Nawroz celebrations. Also common during Nawroz are music concerts with artists from Iran, India, Pakistan and Afghanistan.

Mazar boasts of a women's musical college, something unthinkable elsewhere in the country. Its biggest claim to fame is the sport Buzkashi, which can be seen most weekends, from winter until Nawroz. Buzkashi means "goat dragging" in Persian, and is a sport in which horse-mounted players attempt to drag a goat or calf carcass towards a goal. It is the national sport of Afghanistan and was banned under the Taliban regime.

Training Afghan journalists

I was in Afghanistan to train Afghan journalists on how to write from a gender perspective. I was worried about the assignment as I did not know the working languages, and knew even less about the state of journalism in the country.

I do, however, have experience of working with and training journalists, which is what I did at the third world news agency headquartered in Italy. I have also directed an international agency that provided features written by women journalists, from a gender perspective, to mainstream media and had done trainings in Latin and Central America with instant translation to and from Spanish. But these were all short workshops, not a ten day course. I didn't know how I was going to manage!

I was curious about the students, their qualifications and experience. As my conversations with the NGO had been on the phone and by email, there were information gaps, and I just couldn't form a picture in my mind. I was asked for a training curriculum but I begged off, asking to be allowed to do it when I got to Kabul. I wanted to meet the students, understand the environment and tailor make the curriculum accordingly.

At the training centre I shared a room with four other people—three Afghans and one Belarussian. It was an 8x10 ft. room on the first floor, with large windows overlooking a mosque and some houses with courtyards. To ward off the March cold, there was a sawdust-fuelled bokhari in the centre of the room.

I learned that each of the courses I was to teach would be for two weeks, Sunday to Thursday, for three hours. When the students were not in class, they were receiving hands-on training in print, radio and TV journalism. The training centre had a guest house for students from the provinces. (Administratively, Afghanistan is divided into 34 provinces and 398 districts, with about 1000 villages. Each province has a governor who is appointed by the President.)

On the first day of the first course, I faced ten men and one woman between the ages of 16 to 29, working mostly in radio stations in various provinces of Afghanistan. I was given a translator, Farheen, to work with. I spoke in English and Farheen translated into Dari and/or Pashto. We did an ice-breaking exercise to get to know each other. There was an introduction session where the students participated enthusiastically. They talked about their favourite foods, colours, and songs and, above all, about love. Most of the trainees were single and shy, but curiously excited about the world. They asked me why I had left my family in India and were very appreciative of my being here with them.

As I had suspected, the curriculum would have to be practical. I kept it simple, the concepts intact, but with everyday examples. I started with getting them to understand and develop the male and female sides of their personality as a precursor to understanding gender. Over the two weeks, we talked about the difference between gender and sex, discussed the position and portrayal of women in the media, and looked at selected stories in local media and whether they did or did not have a gender perspective. The students were alert, full of questions, and very concerned about forced marriage, violence against women and the rights of women in Afghanistan.

I wanted to get the students out of the building and give them some field training. So, on March 8, International Women's Day, we made a field trip to the Loya Jirga Tent at the Kabul Polytechnic where President Karzai addressed a gathering, consisting mostly of women. This was the second time I was present at a public meeting being addressed by President Karzai, the last one being during my trip in 2004.

The students were very excited as they took their positions in the media section. None of them had seen the President in person, nor had they interviewed women, face-to-face, before. But, that day, surrounded by almost 2,000 women they interviewed the women, rapidly taking notes or capturing their voices on their mini disc recorders. The next day we reviewed the trip; many said they had never seen so many women in one place, and all so good looking!

People ask me why there weren't more women in the training courses. It could be that five years was not long enough to overturn what had happened to the people of Afghanistan, especially women, in the last two decades. But more women are coming into media now and my goal in the training was to ensure that the male trainees were sensitised to make space for women and defend their rights as colleagues. The women trainees, I hoped, would learn that media is a male-defined and dominated profession and they would need courage and determination to stay in the profession, rise to senior positions and make it attractive for other women in the future.

In 2012, there were about 11,000 local journalists in Afghanistan of whom about 2,500 were women. Many women choose to work in radio, where they are more anonymous than on TV. Those who had joined TV networks as newscasters were threatened by men. There was a view that women could work behind the scenes in media, but must not show their faces on TV. "All the TV networks are in all seriousness asked to stop women presenters from appearing without a veil and with dense make-up," the Information and Culture Ministry said. "All women newscasters on Afghan TV channels are also asked to respect Islamic and Afghan values," it added.[3]

Progress in the media and freedom of expression are generally viewed as the biggest gains of the post-Taliban era in Afghanistan. In 2014, according to the Ministry of Information and Culture, there were more than 75 television stations, one hundred radio stations and hundreds of publications. Under the Taliban in the 1990s, there was one radio station and two newspapers which were used essentially to spread government propaganda.

While the media community is vibrant now, women are still under-represented, which is not that different from the situation in most of South Asia. Many Afghan women were excited when the Taliban regime collapsed, as they stepped out of their homes in huge numbers to study, work, and raise their voices through the media.

According to Dr. Soraya Sobrang, women rights commissioner at Afghanistan's Independent Human Rights Commission, hazardous working environments, cultural barriers, inadequate skills, discriminatory contracts, and sexual harassment have dispersed the interest in, and enthusiasm for, joining the media, that many Afghan women expressed after the fall of the Taliban. Discriminatory contracting policies in many of Afghanistan's media organisations and frequent sexual harassment are also deterring women from working in the media. In most such organisations, employees are subject to a six-month embargo on working for other media outlets when they leave their jobs. Fearing they may be out of work for six months makes female journalists increasingly vulnerable as they are forced to submit to abuse and sexual harassment by media owners and managers.[4]

Picnic on Nawroz

Nawroz, widely celebrated in Afghanistan and by Afghans all over the world, is also known as Farmer's Day, and preparations are made for about two weeks leading up to the first day of the New Year, March 21.

On the eve of Nawroz, special dishes such as Sabzi Challaw (spinach and rice) are cooked to welcome spring and ask for a prosperous crop season. Bakeries make Kulcha-e-Now Rozie, a special rice biscuit decorated with various colours in honour of the holiday. People also make or buy Mahi (fried fish) and Jelabi (fried sugar dessert) which are eaten at picnics. A distinctive sweet called Samanak is made from wheat-germ, and the custom is for women to gather together from late evening to daylight, like a "girls' night in", and prepare the dish, while singing special songs.

Most people celebrate the day by going out on picnics, enjoying the greenery, and especially the tulip flowers that bloom for 24 hours—and then there is kite-flying.

Like the locals, I also went out on a picnic on the day, at the invitation of Federica, a career diplomat at the German embassy. The day before the picnic it rained all day, but on the day itself, it was bright and sunny. I had known Federica in

India and was happily surprised to find her working in Kabul as a gender adviser. A job, she attested, was particularly hard in a culture like Afghanistan.

Federica, her two German colleagues and I headed to Istalif, a hill town about 45 kilometres north of Kabul, stopping only to pick up bread and water. The view changed as we left the city behind us. The roads improved as we passed wheat-fields, mud homes and vineyards. Istalif has been undergoing reconstruction and restoration after being destroyed under Taliban rule. The town is famous for shops specialising in the handmade, glazed Istalif pottery.

We took a dirt road to the left of the highway and reached our destination in about 45 minutes. Parking the vehicle by a stream, we climbed to the top of the hill—a lovely area, with a spectacular view—a bit like Italian hill towns. We saw flowers on the peach and plum trees and a carpet of the famous red, pink and white tulips on the ground.

Thomas Wide, a Kennedy Scholar at Harvard University who lived in Afghanistan in 2007–2008 writes,

> As the great British travel writer Eric Newby raced through Afghanistan to begin his short walk in the Hindu Kush, his guide lamented that they would not be stopping at Istalif en route, and employed an old Afghan proverb about this village perched precariously in the foothills of the Hindu Kush: 'He who has not seen Istalif has seen nothing.'[5]

Wide continues,

> Throughout the region, turquoise-coloured glazes, which have their origins in the pre-Islamic era and had a golden age during the Sassanian and Parthian periods, have remained very popular. Similarly, incised surface decoration made its way eastward to

Istalif

Afghanistan from tenth-century Iran. These innovations had a major influence on smaller pottery centres like Istalif.

William Dalrymple, while describing the glorious history of Istalif in *Return of a King—The Battle for Afghanistan*, says,

> Istalif was always renowned as one of the most beautiful places in Afghanistan. The Emperor Babur fell in love with it in the 16th century and used to hold parties in his rose garden and summer house there. Alexander Burnes, a British political agent to Dost Mohammed in the 19th century, had come here to relax amid the walnut trees. He described the mountain streams as full of fish and the rich orchards and vineyards.
>
> In 1842, following the reoccupation of Kabul, the last

> remnants of the hostile Afghan tribes were a threat to the intended withdrawal. General Pollock sent Major-Gen McCaskill north to Istalif where he defeated the Afghans. Those who did not escape were killed and the town partially destroyed. The British and Indian soldiers set fire to the clothes of their captives and burned them alive. They massacred women and children as well.[6]

Fortunately, we are in a different time and century. On our way, we had children smiling and friendly, waving at us and calling out in English. Two boys, in fact, really took a shine to Federica and me and returned to offer us a boiled egg! A group of girls shyly came over to where we were sitting and handed us a plastic bag with some bread and something we didn't recognise. Our picnic food consisted of cheese, sausages, naan, keenus and dates. We took pictures, exchanged stories, laughed, and admired the landscape.

As we headed back to the car, a family tucking into biryani and making tea over a stove, offered us Haft Mewa—a Nawroz specialty prepared from seven different dried fruits and nuts, served in their own juices. These are red raisins, black raisins, yellow raisins, *senjid* (the dried fruit of the oleaster tree), pistachio, dried apricot, and dried apple. Often walnuts, almonds and other dried fruit are also added. (See recipe below).

We chatted briefly with the family and left, making a detour to the village of Istalif and its one-street commercial area with a few shops for everyday essentials. We shopped for pottery, special cookies and cream puffs, which Federica insisted were famous for their delicate taste.

I was particularly taken by the pottery. The glazes were earth colours—deep brown, mustard and green, with the exception of the turquoise coloured creations. An old man with a white beard and warm eyes served us, and was indulgent as we gushed over the plates, cups, jugs, platters, bowl and mugs.

As we drove back, Federica received a call from an Afghan colleague who invited her over to their home for Nawroz. She explained that she was with a group and was promptly asked to bring all of us along. We stopped at the Kabul market to pick up a box of sweets for the family. Jawed and his family welcomed us, offered haft mewa and other sweets.

Back at the guest house, as I prepared to go to bed, I reflected on how fortunate I was to be in the country on New Year's Day.

Istalif pottery platter

Tulips from Istalif

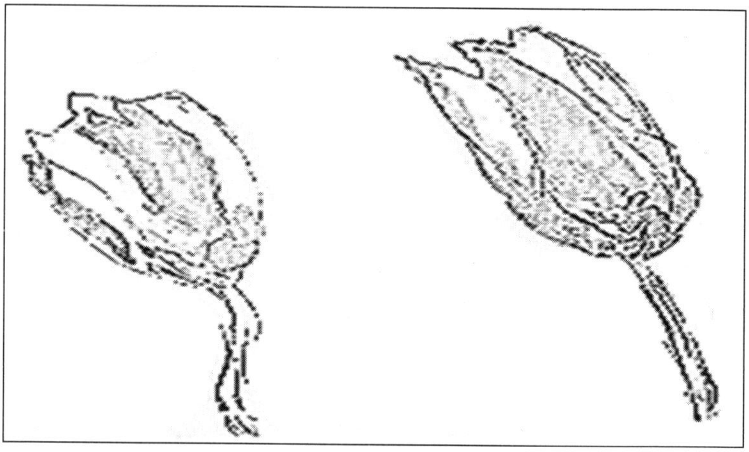

I arranged the Istalif pottery around the room, put the plucked tulips in a small vase and photographed them. Next morning, sitting outside on the verandah, I did a water colour of them.

For those of you who may be interested in preparing Haft Mewa, here is a recipe. Do try it.

Haft Mewa (serves 6)

3/4 cup walnuts
½ cup pistachios
½ cup yellow raisins
1 cup red raisins
½ cup dried red cherries
1 cup dried apricots
½ cup blanched, slivered almonds
½ tsp. rose water (optional)
5 cups cold water
Large lidded container with a wide mouth

Blanch the walnuts and pistachios. Bring 3 cups of water to a boil, remove from the heat, add the walnuts and pistachios, cover and let it sit for 20 minutes. In a large bowl add both kinds of raisins, cherries and apricots. Rinse three times in cold water to remove any residue.

When the nuts are ready, pour the hot water out and add cold water. Peel the skin off the nuts.

Add the dried fruit and the nuts to the container along with the rose water and 5 cups of cold water. Stir well. The water should be at least one inch above the ingredients. Refrigerate for 2–4 days. The longer you leave the mixture the sweeter it gets. It will keep in the fridge for up to 7 days.

Serve the haft mewa in a bowl with its juices. It goes well with vanilla or mango ice cream or plain yogurt.

A ghazal concert

The highlight of my last two weeks was the Jagjit Singh concert. On that day, he sang for about three hours to an almost full house at the Loya Jirga Tent at Kabul University Polytechnic. He told stories, cracked jokes, and encouraged the audience to clap along with certain ghazals, and they loved all of it.

I also met him in person at a reception in his honour ahead of the concert, as a guest of Federica, and thought how ordinary and vulnerable he looked—with his dyed hair, gold chain, black sweater with a stretched collar and jeans and loafers. The next evening, I was marvelling at his extraordinary transformation as he took full command of the audience.

Six of my colleagues and housemates who did not understand either Hindi or Urdu also came to the concert and joined in the spirit of the evening.

Ghazals are songs of love and loss, based on poetry

consisting of rhyming couplets and a refrain. They are believed to have originated in 6th century Arabic verse and came to Asia in the 12th century, brought here by Sufi mystics. Originally part of the poetry in Dari and Urdu, ghazals today are part of many of the Indian subcontinent's languages. They are very popular in Afghanistan. Besides Jagjit Singh, Afghans have their own heroes in Ahmad Walia (who lives in Germany) and Farhad Darya.

The teaching experience

In one of my classes, there was a new love poem on the white board almost every day. The trainees were keen to read it and got Farheen to translate it into English. Sometimes, they attempted to translate it themselves.

They called me Ustad and, sometimes, 'teacher'. They had a curiosity about life and were very affectionate, often expressing their gratitude and surprise at my leaving my husband, child and home for three months to be able to teach them.

At the end of each two week session, there was an evaluation and a wrap-up where certificates were given, photographs taken, and goodbyes said. I took the first batch I taught for lunch at the local restaurant, 'Herat' after a field trip, and we all had platefuls of biryani and kebabs. In the end, they surprised me with a necklace and a scarf.

For the second batch, on the last day of class, I brought fruit and nut cake, coconut cookies, and cold drinks. The trainees read out their messages to me and Farheen translated them. I came with no expectations and ended up with something truly special. Every class was different and surprising, and all questions challenged and delighted me.

The brunch at Kabul Serena

For Kabulites, and those who can afford it, Friday brunch at the five-star Kabul Serena Hotel, is a much vaunted experience. I heard many expats, including my housemates, talk about the great food you could get for US $25.

I was curious but hesitatant about patronising a five-star hotel in a conflict-ridden country. However, it was one of the few places that my expat friends who worked in embassies could go to for security reasons, so I agreed to meet them there one Friday.

Aziz dropped me off around 11:30 a.m., as that's when the group was gathering. It was a farewell of sorts for several friends of Brenda, my Canadian friend, who were leaving Afghanistan. Crossing security checks, I came into a beautiful reception area from where I could see the swimming pool. My four brunch companions were already seated at a table in the open, next to the dining area where the buffet was laid out. There was a delicious aroma of grilled meats—chicken, beef and lamb. After greeting each other, we moved indoors towards the brunch tables.

To the left was the sushi bar, then the omelette area, followed by the pasta section, all fresh. In the middle aisle were salads and desserts. To the far end were the hot foods. To the right were the juices and fresh fruits, and in between the food, were decorations made of fruits and vegetables that were floating in glass jars, adding to the atmosphere. It was a visual delight.

In between many rounds of food and desserts, I noticed that many of the people I had seen on my way in had already left. Most tables had groups of five-six people, much like ours. There was laughter and talking, people greeting each other. Kabul's expat development community is not that large.

It was 3:00 p.m. and the sun had moved across the sky, towards the west. We asked for the bill. Each of us paid $25, which included the tip. The service had been excellent, with well-trained and cheerful staff. We took a slow walk through the ground floor of the hotel stopping to ooh and aah at the pastry shop and bar. My phone rang—Aziz had arrived to pick me up. I kissed my friends goodbye and left.

Picnic in Shamali valley

Friday being a holiday, we decided to go on a picnic to Shamali, which means north, in Dari.

The Shamali valley's fertile plains produce grapes, almonds and walnuts. It is a strategic geographical location and serves as a buffer and link between the Hindu Kush mountains and Kabul city. Because of its location, it was the frontline battleground throughout Afghanistan's long history of conflict. The area was densely mined and constant clashes between the warring factions resulted in the majority of the Shamali population fleeing their homes to seek refuge in Kabul or overseas.

We were going to the house that Mir, an Afghan-German, was building on his acreage. The weather seemed like it couldn't make up its mind—sunny and cloudy, alternatively. Federica and some of us collected at Mir's house in the middle of Kabul and began to drive north in four vehicles, and were at his place in 45 minutes. Mir offered to show us the partially finished house that was being built as a mixture of traditional architecture with modern touches, with impeccable taste in the choice of building material, fixtures and interiors.

Mir, like many other Afghans, sought refuge in Germany

during the Communist and Taliban years. In 2001, he returned to set up a media centre and a restaurant. He represented one of the new faces of Afghanistan—rooted in culture, exposed to the world, and committed to building a country that is relevant in the 21st century.

As we moved to the picnic area, I saw that in an open and almost flat space, a giant yellow, green and red *khamya* (tent) had been erected, supported with five tall bamboo poles—one at each corner and one in the middle. On the ground, a dozen or so kilims had been spread, with soft mattresses and bolsters. A woman in black was preparing to make bolani—crepes stuffed with potato (see bolani recipe below). A small wood fire had just been started. There was a three-generation Afghan family present, and I learnt that some of the young people lived in the Netherlands and were visiting for their grandmother's funeral.

At a distance, I saw the Kuchis with their pitched tents, sheep and donkeys. Kuchi is nomad in Dari, and they are Pashtuns from southern and eastern Afghanistan. Though traditionally nomadic, many have settled in north-west Afghanistan, after strong encouragement by the Taliban government in an area that was traditionally occupied by Uzbeks and Tajiks. Only a few thousands still follow their traditional livelihood of nomadic herding, while others are farmers, or settled in cities or have immigrated. The largest population of Kuchi is probably in Registan, the desert in southern Afghanistan.

Due to their nomadic lifestyle, the Kuchis were never really involved in Afghan politics but played a key role in Afghanistan's post-Taliban political revival. Together with the Pashtun, they supported President Karzai in the 2005 presidential elections. They were given their own constituency and allocated 10 of the 249 seats in the new National Assembly, seven for men and three for women. Kuchis were also promised a government department to handle their affairs, but it has yet to materialise.

We sat on the kilims and did what is normally done at picnics—we talked. Soon, green tea arrived in glass mugs, followed by bolani and steaming dishes of kebab, kichri (rice and lentils), a fresh salad with tomatoes, cucumbers and green onions, kofta curry and naan. My friends and I had carried a box of local sweets, which soon attracted flies. There were jokes made about Tom, a member of our group, who had never had a day's stomach problem in Kabul, but on a recent trip suffered from food poisoning in Washington DC! I talked to an Afghan woman who had returned after 30 years to try and start a women and children's' health project, frustrated and tired at how slowly things move in the country. There are other Afghans like her and Mir who were in exile for years. After 2001, they returned to Afghanistan but were left disillusioned at how things work or do not work in the country.

The wind came up, trying to take the *khamya* away. There was loud thunder and some raindrops. We picked up the water bottles, plates, cups, and our personal belongings. While some headed for walks, I opted to wait in the car to avoid the dust blowing around. A German in his mid-60s also took shelter in the car. As we chatted, he showed me photographs of his family in Afghanistan in the late 1950s—his father had been posted in Afghanistan as an engineer. "It was a different time then," he said. Now retired, he would like to set up a business in Afghanistan.

As we headed back to the city, the sky was dark and beautiful. It continued to rain, but not hard—just enough to settle the dust.

Recipe for Bolani Katachalu (potato)[7]

Bolani is a flatbread and can be stuffed and baked with either spinach, pumpkin, red potato, or green lentil. It is usually served warm and as a side-dish, appetiser, or even as a main dish.

Dough ingredients

3 ½ cups all-purpose flour
1 cup water, room temperature
1 tsp salt
1 tsp olive oil

Filling ingredients

2 medium potatoes
1/2 cup chopped fresh coriander
1/2 cup chopped scallions (white and green parts)
2 tbsp olive oil
1 ½ tsp salt
1 tsp ground black pepper

For frying: 1/4 cup cooking oil

Yogurt sauce

1 cup plain yogurt
2 tbsp water
1 garlic clove, minced
1 tsp dried dill
1/4 tsp coriander
1/2 tsp salt

Method

Dough

Mix flour and salt together. Gradually (while mixing) add in water and oil until dough forms a ball. If the dough is too dry, add more water, one tbsp at a time. Knead dough for 10 minutes. Place dough in lightly oiled bowl, cover with a cloth, and let it rest for one hour.

Filling

Scrub potatoes, place in a pot, cover with 2 inches cold water, add a good pinch of salt, and bring to a boil over high heat. After boiling for 20 minutes, check to see if the potatoes are done. Smaller potatoes may get done sooner than larger ones. Once the potatoes are done, drain them and let sit for 5-10 minutes. Peel and quarter the potatoes. Mash with 2 tbsp. olive oil, salt, and pepper. Add the fresh coriander and scallions and continue mashing.

Assembling and cooking

Take a portion of the dough (about the size of a small apple) and roll it into a smooth ball. Spread some flour onto your surface, and roll the ball with a rolling pin. The dough should be as thin and be about 10–12 inch in diameter. The thinner, the better!

Spread a little more than 1/4 cup of the filling on one half of the dough, leaving about 1/4 inch border around the rim.

Fold the dough in half over the filling and press to seal. If necessary, continue pressing and flattening the bolani to remove any excess air inside the pocket.

Heat 1/4 cup olive oil in a pan. The oil should be hot enough that the bolani sizzles when placed in the pan. Brown the bolani, two at a time, until golden and crisp on both sides. This will only take a couple minutes on each side.

Place cooked bolani on a paper towel or plate as they finish. Add more oil to your pan as needed while you cook the rest.

Serve warm with the yogurt sauce made of plain yogurt, garlic, dill, coriander, and salt.

Bagh-e-Babur (The gardens of Babur)

On another Friday, we chose to go to Babur's garden or Bagh-e Babur—a historic park which also houses Babur's tomb. In his memoirs, the *Baburnama*, are details of the 'avenue garden' in Kabul, dating back to 1528 AD.

The garden was a ten-minute drive from my house in Karte-seh. Federica, a few friends and I drove into the garden grounds and instantly felt a drop in the temperature. With its large open space, trees and bushes which swayed gently with the breeze, and fountains, the garden provided an idyllic setting for picnics. Federica and our group walked around and she stopped to greet several people and introduce them to us—Rory Stewart, of the Turquoise Mountain Foundation and Ratish Nanda, the Indian architect with the Aga Khan Trust for Culture, who was on the team overseeing the redevelopment of the garden.

Bagh-e-Babur has changed drastically from the Mughal design of the space to the present, with external influences shaping the use of the site. For example, the Aga Khan Historic Cities Programme describes how by 1880, Amir Abdu Rahman Khan constructed a pavilion and a residence for his wife, Bibi Halima. In 1933, the area was converted into a public recreation space with pools and fountains becoming the central focal point. A modern greenhouse and swimming pool were added in the late 1970s. Currently, a renovated enclosure molded with the same marble used for the Taj Mahal, fabricated in India and transported to Afghanistan via Iran, surrounds the tomb.

I moved on to the other end of the garden and saw several

young men enjoying and partaking in a cock fight. We exchanged pleasantries and they happily posed for my camera. You could see Afghan families walking, talking and children playing. The setting was beautiful and almost surreal. It was easy to forget that we were in a conflict-ridden country, that at this very moment, somewhere there would be gunfire exchanged, soldiers getting killed, loss of lives and property, and people who continue to suffer.

Over the next week, there were changes in my guest house, as the green trees burst forth with blossoms, indicating the beginning of warmer times. As I stood on my very generous terrace, I saw that my neighbours across the street, a Danish de-mining NGO, had moved out and taken their large and very noisy generator with them, making my life much quieter. Without all that noise, the snow-covered mountains I could see from my terrace looked all the more serene.

Building youth leadership

As a part of a five-member jury, I participated in the Youth Leaders Forum sponsored by the Friedrich Ebert Stiftung (FES), a German political foundation promoting social, political and economic development, active in Afghanistan since 2002.

My job there was to assist in shortlisting the group, from 40 to 20. The group had young men and women between the ages of 16 to 31 and included students, lawyers, medical doctors, teachers, researchers, administrators, members of political parties, print journalists and radio and TV announcers.

The assessment process had participants collecting signatures of people to evaluate their entrepreneurial spirit, followed by group work, where they discussed the attributes of a good and bad minister by role playing, talk shows and some speeches. In the group session I noticed men and women working together, sharing ideas, women sitting together, stating their opinions, firmly and gently.

After tea and coffee, they spoke about something or someone that has inspired them and finally a 25-minute writing assignment, choosing between two topics—how the government can improve security, or how they would evaluate parliament's performance. While deciding the list of shortlisted candidates, there was a spoken understanding that more women would be selected, as they have had fewer advantages than men.

I looked at the participants, speaking in Dari and English, animated, shy, articulate, eager, and uncertain, talking among themselves during break and lunch, and felt pleased and hopeful about the future of Afghanistan.

A reminder of the struggle that the country and these youngsters faced came the same morning, with news of fighting in the southern provinces of Kandahar, Helmand and Uruzgan, which border Pakistan. Helmand has a large Pashtun population (92 per cent), who are primarily members of the Durrani and Ghilzai tribes. The Taliban and its allies have a strong presence here, and the area has witnessed some of the most frequent and violent clashes between the insurgents and coalition forces in recent years.

These three provinces are also the largest opium-producing areas in the world. In 2011, the United Nations Office on Drugs and Crime (UNODC) estimated that 131,000 hectares of opium were under cultivation in Afghanistan; by 2014, this figure had risen to an estimated 224,000 hectares.[8]

Insurgency and opium are a few of the many challenges facing the government. The task of keeping peace and ensuring a drug-free economy is daunting. However, a strong youth leadership is not just necessary, but also rewarding and a constructive means to ensure these goals are met.

Zamestan, Bahar and Tabestan: the changing seasons

I came to Kabul in the season of *zamestan* (winter), enjoyed the eagerly awaited *bahar* (spring) and then complained about *tabestan* (summer). And, in this time, Kabul moved from brown to green. Winter, with its clear blue skies, snow-capped mountains in the distance, bright sun, and stark trees and bushes, slowly gave way to cloudy skies, dust storms, and trees and bushes full of green leaves.

Outside my first floor room and terrace, there was a white rose creeper, intertwined with a grapevine, full of green leaves. The pomegranate trees are bursting with buds. Two weeks ago, going to work at about 9:00 a.m., I spied an older man with a full salt and pepper beard, sunglasses, a straw hat, on a ladder trimming the pomegranate trees and the grapevines. On enquiring about him, I was told that he was the man who trimmed the grapevines. By the time I returned, the same man had engineered quite the transformation of the garden, replacing the overgrown aspect of the garden with sharply trimmed creepers and trim grapevines.

Roses had bloomed all over Kabul, but the hot season had arrived.

The shops in the markets have draped plastic over their fronts to keep out the fierce sun. Push-carts sell a yogurt-based drink (*doh*) in large mud vats, covered with leaves to keep the temperatures down. Others sell rhubarb, which Afghans eat raw like a salad. There is sugarcane—cut in small pieces—that brought back my childhood memories of India. My father loved sugarcane and we bought it in bunches, right off the fields. On our visits to Punjab, where my parents grew up, my cousins would teach my sisters and me to bite the shell of the sugarcane with our bare teeth and suck the juice.

On my street, watermelons appeared overnight in the shops and a shopkeeper installed an ice cream-making machine and offered wafer cones. The shop turned out to be a hit with children and grown-ups. Coats, mufflers, shawls and boots gave way to lighter summer garments and sandals. Children ran around the streets, playing ball and having a good time.

The almost-summer night sky in Kabul is beautiful, the moon, stars and clouds are all magical. There is a profusion of colours—orange, grey and pink, against the mountains. The breeze is soft, keeping the temperatures down during the night.

And so, it is *bahar* in the night and *tabestan* in the day.

Falling in love

May—my third month in Kabul and walking down the streets a few days ago, I realised I had fallen in love with Afghanistan.

I knew most of the shopkeepers and several residents on the street I was living on. I would always stop to greet them and exchange salaams no matter how much of a hurry I was in. I loved watching the children—skipping to school with their backpacks. They learn English in school, and greet you with a polite hello. Little palms are held up in a high five, or a simple handshake. I loved their smiles, red cheeks, and shining eyes. Girls wore black pants and long black blouses with a white scarf. They are quite stunning, standing out as they walk alone, or in twos and threes. Many boys snake around on their bikes, on the street which has been dug up ever since I got here.

Women in burqas, older men in front of the mosque or just

the workers on the street, everyone readily responded to my salaam with a smile.

I loved my students; they were attentive, curious, and well behaved. Besides being regular journalists, they were poets and philosophers. I looked at them and wondered how a country with so many years of war and devastation could produce young people with such little malice, anger or hurt. They appeared calm and untroubled, mature beyond their age. When I shared this with expat friends, one said that it is possible they are this way because they had no childhood. Given the situation of war and conflict in Afghanistan since the late 1980s, this is probably true.

Afghan children suffered during the civil wars fought among different factions between 1989 and 2001, when many were recruited into militias.[9] They were kidnapped and sold as "terrorists" by members of the Northern Alliance to the US Special Forces, for $5,000 each. According to some reports, they were imprisoned for years in Guantanamo Bay and in secret prisons in Afghanistan. They were forced into armies, the police force, and militias. The United Nations Children's Fund (UNICEF) reported from Kabul on June 24, 2004 that 2,205 children between the ages of 14–18 had been demobilized; it also reported that there may be as many as 8,000 remaining child soldiers, police, and militiamen.

Despite these horrors, the students in my classes were polite, respectful and wanted to learn.

I loved the open markets that sold anything and everything, from dried fruits and nuts to fresh vegetables and fruits, textiles, recycled and new clothes, shoes and sandals. The open market in Polisar, a five-minute drive from my house in south-west Kabul, was a pleasure to walk through. There were large open sacks of various varieties of rice—local and from Pakistan; lentils, bird-feed, flour, sugar, and dried fruits. Push-carts that were heaped with fruits and vegetables, and fresh cheese adorned with green leaves to keep the flies off. There was also a vendor there who made *bulyani*—a crepe filled with leeks.

I loved the mountains, the blue of the sky, the brightness of the moon and stars, and the houses on the mountain that lit up at night. I loved feeling the gentle cool breeze on my skin. Most of all, I loved that I could try and make a difference in a country that is being created almost from scratch. I felt useful, wanted and loved. Afghanistan has made me fall in love with its sites, its people, its food, its culture and its optimism for a better future.

My favourite restaurant

My favourite restaurant in Kabul is La Fontaine, a place I stumbled onto purely by accident. I arrived in Kabul on a Tuesday and by Friday (the first holiday), I had persuaded my housemate, Aleksandr to join me on a trip to Flower and Chicken Streets, as I was keen to meet and greet the people I had met two years ago when I lived there.

Several hours later, hungry, I suggested that we look for a Chinese restaurant I had eaten in on my last trip. As we walked around, we saw several groups of people and cars in front of La Fontaine. Though we were told that lunch was not being served, Aleksandr and I walked in and were greeted by a large garden and a charming house. We met Dan, the owner, who apologised and said he wasn't serving lunch that day. A slim, greying man of average height who wore glasses and had an infectious smile, Dan suggested we come back for dinner, and offered us some delicious chocolates he had made that morning.

I went back to La Fontaine many times. The décor is traditional Afghan embroidered curtains, kilims on the floor, and wooden tables with white tablecloths. The yellow chairs have coir matting on the backs and seats, and soft cushions. In winter, there was a bokhari as you walked into the restaurant. As the weather changed, Dan placed tables on the verandah and the garden.

Dan and I became friends and he never failed to stop by my table. He is originally from France and worked in the corporate sector till he left his job to, as he says, "live a little more dangerously". We talked about the challenges of working and living in Afghanistan, especially Kabul, and reminisced about Myanmar, a country we both loved. He is full of stories that never failed to make me laugh, about running businesses in different countries and his earlier life.

The food at La Fontaine is a mixture of continental and Afghan—steaks, pizzas, ravioli, cannelloni, salads, soups and lobster. The bread is delicious and offered on the house with the meal. The bakery is behind the restaurant, and many people come by for baguette, salt bread, grissini and croissants. Dan also offers great desserts—chocolate mousse, almond and lemon pies, heavy and light chocolate cakes, meringue—which he serves with custard.

One night, Grace, a friend from Australia, and I sat under the trees. The sky got darker, and the moon and stars came out. Dan joined us at our table, offering us a glass of red wine and telling tales. I admired his haircut and Grace and I complained about ours. He said he got his from the barber at the Mustafa Hotel. "Only for men", he said with a smile.

La Fontaine is about Dan, who has lived in China, Vietnam, Myanmar and now, Afghanistan. It is about a space which is comforting, warm and welcoming, with an ambience that brings people together. In Kabul, expats have limited places to relax in. Dan and other expats have either come to Afghanistan to set up businesses, especially restaurants and cafes. But there are challenges. For one, expats can only invest 49 per cent in any business, they must have local partners. And, as in all partnerships, sooner or later there are situations which demand patience and experience in dealing with the local culture. With limited or sometimes no systems in place, this can be quite challenging.

Creating health for Afghans

A field trip with the students in my journalism and reproductive health class had us heading north to Mir Bacha Kot to visit a health clinic. We started from the training centre in two small buses and stopped to pick up Samira, the Director of the Afghan Institute for Learning (AIL), and the organisation that runs the clinic. AIL is an Afghan women-run NGO founded in 1995 by Dr. Sakena Yacoobi, to offer education and health services to Afghans, especially women and children. Started at refugee camps in Pakistan where there were no educational opportunities, the AIL operated 80 'secret schools' for 3,000 girls in Afghanistan during the Taliban regime and also trained teachers. Since 2001, AIL has expanded a great deal, opening learning centres requested by communities, establishing clinics and running workshops and trainings in many subjects.

Forty-five minutes' drive north of Kabul and we arrived at the Shamali Valley. Though the distance is hardly 20 kilometres, we encountered a fair amount of traffic. As we squeezed our way around a larger van in the clinic's driveway, we saw 50 men, women and children in a partially covered courtyard. Inside, there were posters of the human anatomy and displays of various contraceptives on the wall in the 8x10' well-lit family planning counselling room. The nurse explained the services offered and the problems that women came with. Outside, women waited patiently with health cards in their hands.

Samira invited the students to the exam room where a mother had brought a week-old baby, with an infected navel. The students were fascinated, gathering around, full of questions, scribbling in their note pads as I watched the mother swaddle the baby.

The entire staff of Mir Bacha Kot lives in Kabul. They leave the city every morning to get to the clinic by 7:00 a.m. The clients are local women and children who come from 8:00 a.m. to 12:00 p.m. For men, the clinic timings are 12:00 p.m. to 4:00 p.m. Despite the high demand, the clinic can serve only 200 patients a day as it wants to offer quality care.

On the way back from Mir Bacha Kot, Samira showed us where she was born and went to a local school for a year before shifting to Kabul. The area is called River of Milk and Yogurt, after a community that keeps goats and makes yogurt. Samira studied law in Pakistan, but was drawn to the health sector and switched fields. With three children under the age of five, her husband is an almost-doctor, having shifted to computers when he was just a year short of completing his medical degree. Samira had hoped he would complete his medical education and work as a doctor. "There is so much to do in Afghanistan", she says.

Beginning in 1979, the military conflict destroyed the health system of the country. Most medical professionals left the country by 1992, and all medical training programmes ceased. The drought of 1999–2002 exacerbated the conditions even further, leaving an estimated 800,000 Afghans disabled.

In 2003, there were only 11 physicians and 18 nurses left for every 100,000 people, and the per capita health expenditure was just US $28. Additionally, there was only one medical facility for every 27,000 people in 2004, and some centres were responsible for as many as 300,000 people. With a decrepit health infrastructure and an estimated one-quarter of the population without any access to health care, international organisations became the primary health care providers and also started the process to rebuild the healthcare system.[10]

Lack of a safe and functional healthcare system in Afghanistan has meant that women and children are the worst sufferers. Afghanistan has the worlds' second highest maternal mortality rate, and the highest infant and child mortality rate. However, according to a 2012 report by Save the Children things are looking up—improved healthcare and the rise of women attending school have made Afghanistan move up from its position as the worst place on earth to be a mother. "More mothers are surviving and fewer children are dying, and this is something we need to be celebrating", said Charlotte Maranto, advocacy and mobilisation senior manager at Save the Children in Kabul. Nonetheless, despite the improvements in healthcare, about 275 children die every day in a country of 25 million.

As we leave, the sun is in the middle of the sky. It's hot and the students suggest we stop for *dogha*—a local drink made with yogurt, cucumbers, salt and pepper. On a hot day, this is most welcome.

World Press Freedom Day

The celebration of World Press Freedom Day, on May 20th, saw some hundred people, including ministers and their deputies, journalists and members of the international community, gather together in the garden of a downtown hotel, Carwan Sarai, under a very colourful tent, a shining sun and clear, blue skies.

Of the three-hour function, the most interesting speaker was the *New York Times* correspondent, Carlotta Gall, who has worked in Afghanistan and Pakistan for many years. A seasoned journalist, simply yet elegantly dressed, she took the podium and made a no-nonsense speech on the challenges of working in Afghanistan. She highlighted the physical threat that continues to prevail, owing to the war in the south and revealed that she herself had come close to a suicide bomb a few weeks earlier. She cited the lack of transparency and the tendency to fudge facts by the establishment, the American coalition troops and the other parties, including the Taliban, as a real problem in reporting stories.

For both international and local media in Afghanistan, journalism is a challenging profession. Press releases issued by the ministries are often incorrect and inconvenient facts covered up. Police are told not to speak to the press. When the government is criticised, they tend to form a commission, promising to look into issues; after a while, other concerns become more pressing and the issues are forgotten.

Journalists have to work really hard to get stories, and there are real dangers in exposing vested interests, warlords, opium growers, traffickers and other anti-social elements. Journalists are threatened, beaten up and often simply disappear.

The minister of information and culture said freedom of the press is a heady experience. "We can make mistakes and get excited. But we must not offend, defame or personalise."

Seeds of hope: Documenting change

The Afghan Constitution guarantees that "from each province, on average, at least two female delegates shall have membership to the Wolesi Jirga", thereby guaranteeing 68 seats (27 per cent) in the 249 member Wolesi Jirga, the lower house, to women. Similarly, the Afghan election law contains a provision that at least 25 per cent of seats in the provincial councils must be reserved for women.

Overall, the performance of women in the 2005 elections was surprisingly strong, both in the Wolesi Jirga and the provincial councils. Nineteen women (just under ten per cent of all parliamentarians) won enough votes to be elected without the help of the quota in 2005.[11]

The Afghan Results and Evaluation Unit (AREU) reported that another surprising aspect of this strong performance was that it was not as geographically focused as expected. Women won seats in 18 provinces, representing every region of Afghanistan. Even in the more conservative Pashtun provinces of the east, south-east and south, some female candidates were able to win non-quota seats, although these were fewer in number than in other regions.

Documenting these changes in Afghanistan is the documentary, *Seeds of Hope*, made by two filmmakers. Imagine two women—one who runs a women-only gym and the other who is a radio newsreader, who fought and won the parliamentary elections in 2005. Fawzia Gailani, exiled for many years in Iran, returned to Afghanistan and opened a gym in the north-west province of Herat, which shares a border with Iran; and Parwin Mohmand, a 40-year-old mother with four children, travelled all over the country to win one of the three Kuchi parliamentary seats. Gailani, a 32-year old with six children won with 16,885 votes in Herat. This was more than any other candidate in the Herat province, and more than any other woman in Afghanistan. Only 20 men nationwide got more votes.

Both women are the protagonists of *Seeds of Hope*, a documentary by Brigitte Brault and Jamila Emami. Brault, a French citizen, came to Afghanistan in 2002 to train Afghan camerawomen. With Emami, one of her fourteen students, they formed a production company called Women's Eyes in 2005. The camera follows Gailani as she goes about her work and fulfils her political duties. Between shots of Afghan women in full garb on exercise machines at Gailani's gym, and her in Parliament, it is an astonishing and refreshing portrayal. Gailani has moved to the capital, Kabul and, as per the norm, has been assigned personal bodyguards to protect her.

In the documentary, Mohmand is seen in conversation with Kuchi male leaders who welcome her as an equal. As the Kuchis are a nomadic community who rely on animals to make a living, the talk is mostly about their need for land to graze their cattle, without having to pay for it. In managing to capture Mohmand on the camera, Brault and Emami go where others have feared to tread, as the Kuchis do not like to have their women photographed. Emami says it took them a month to get the men to agree to a one-day shoot!

We witness the daily chores of the Kuchi women—drawing water from the well, making cheese, stitching and rebuilding the mud wall of a kitchen, while men sit around and watch. When asked why they do not help the women, they say that "it is women's work, we work outside". Women express their aspirations and frustrations—they want mobile health vans, education for their children, and land to settle on as they are tired of moving around.

Both women representatives know that the people who voted for them have high expectations, especially women. *Seeds of Hope* was screened in Kabul on May 21, World Day for Cultural Diversity and Development. It was funded by UNESCO and is in Dari, with English subtitles. Other than the continuous, slightly jarring voiceover, the film is a visual delight, and an important documentation of the change in Afghanistan—a change for the better.

Hul Gil: a harsh reality

With its bright red colour, velvety texture, and tall, upright stem the poppy is a stunningly beautiful flower. Looking at it swaying in the breeze, it is hard to imagine that something so lovely could cause such grief.

In 2005, Afghanistan produced 87 per cent of the world's poppy, and of the country's total population of 25 million, 920,000 were estimated to be drug users in 2006. These figures stand out more as ninety-nine per cent of Afghans are Muslims; according to Islam, all drugs used as intoxicants *(khan)* are forbidden *(haram),* as they cloud the mind and distract from the path of God.

In these conditions, it is complicated to report on drug-related issues. I taught a course on 'Dealing with Drugs' to a class of students between the ages of sixteen and thirty-five, mostly radio journalists from provinces with high opium cultivation. When I asked them if they knew someone addicted to drugs—a friend, an uncle, a neighbour, or a cousin—all hands went up. In the last thirty years Afghans have faced war, conflict, insurgency and terrorism leading to devastation of land and agriculture, large scale exile, and people being forced to be on the move constantly. Such huge changes in their lives and livelihood have naturally led to a great many of them suffering from PTSD (Post Traumatic Stress Disorder).

When the Taliban were in power from 1996 to 2001, they banned poppy cultivation, but they could not stop the smuggling of harvests from previous years. And once the Taliban was defeated, farmers went back to cultivating poppy.

In 2005, an Opium Survey conducted by the Afghan Ministry of Counter Narcotics and the United Nations Office on Drugs and Crime (UNODC) reported that there had been a decline in opium poppy cultivation since 2001 and the area devoted to drug crops had dropped by 21 per cent.

The reason poppy cultivation is extremely popular in Afghanistan is its harsh topography, where growing poppy is not only easier than some other crops, but also one that guarantees a high yield and a big market. According to the 2005 Survey, indicative gross income from opium per hectare was US $5,400, while it was only US $550 from wheat.

Since 2002, there has been an aggressive war against drugs based on the assumption that rule of law and sustainable economic development can make a difference. There are campaigns asking Afghans to not engage in any form of cultivation, manufacture, trafficking and use of drugs.

According to the 2014 Afghanistan Opium Survey published by the Ministry of Counter Narcotics and the United Nations Office on Drugs and Crime, the total area used for poppy cultivation in Afghanistan was estimated at 224,000 hectares. In 2005, it was 104,000 hectares and in 1994, during the time of the Taliban, 71,000 hectares. The vast majority (89 per cent) of opium cultivation takes place in nine provinces in Afghanistan's southern and western regions, which include the country's most insecure provinces. Helmand remains

Afghanistan's major opium-cultivating province, followed by Kandahar, Farah, and Nangarhar.

For nearly 14 years, the Afghan government, with the help of the international community and aid agencies, has worked to eradicate opium production entirely. The 2014 Survey shows that not only have these efforts been unsuccessful, but that the eradication programmes may actually have pushed farmers to increase their outputs. Given the gruelling ecological and socio-economic conditions, it will be some time before there is a substantial change in Afghanistan's opium economy.

Afghanistan, Myanmar, Mexico, and Colombia account for nearly all of opium's underground production, with Afghanistan alone representing roughly 90 per cent of the total output. Based on the 2014 Survey, the farm-gate value for Afghan farmers for cultivating the crop stands at $850 million, compared to $400 million in 2009. Given that the industry is valued at $60 billion a year, by far the largest amount of money is still being made outside the country.

Iran, Afghanistan and Pakistan are the most affected by illicit trade. Two major corridors—the Balkan Route and the Northern Route—are used to transport Afghan opium to international markets. The Balkan Route sees opium move to Iran via Pakistan, before travelling west through Turkey and Greece, ultimately reaching Western Europe. The Northern Route moves opium mainly through northern Afghanistan into Central Asia for the Russian market.

In my class, I saw my students grapple with the personal, political, economic and social dimensions of opium and drugs. They are the new generation, the change-makers. A sixteen year old student asked me how opium came into being, from where, and why is it in Afghanistan? Legend has it that the opium poppy has been around for a long time. Three thousand years before Christ, the Sumerians referred to it as *Hul Gil* or the 'joy plant'. Unfortunately, the joy plant is now the source of misery for millions around the world.

Teachers' Day

May 25 is celebrated as Teachers' Day in Afghanistan. As I entered the training centre and popped inside my translator's room to say salaam, I noticed the roses kept in a glass mug on his desk.

As per schedule, I was taking my drugs class to see a facility of the National Drug Control Police in our neighbourhood of Karte-seh. Four staff members from the UN Office on Drugs and Crime came to accompany us to the facility. Before that though, in my reproductive health class, one student had given me a rose that I also placed in a glass mug on my desk.

The next day, in the drugs class, I got a special speech from the students thanking me for being their teacher, and telling me how much they enjoyed the class, and how grateful they were that I had come from India to teach them. A similar speech was made in the afternoon's reproductive health class. What was unsaid was the love in their eyes, and their smiles. I have two degrees in education, but I had never considered myself a teacher. Though we are addressed as trainers here, my students call me Ustad—the Dari word for teacher.

Learning Dari

The last time I learnt a language was in 1986 when I moved to Italy. A three-month crash course in Italian then enabled me to buy vegetables, book a double room on the phone, ask the Rome railway inquiry desk about the cost of a round-trip ticket to Florence, communicate with the Italian telex operators in my news agency, and order food from a menu.

In my third week in Kabul, as Aleksandr and I were riding in a shared car, asking Aziz, our driver, how to say this and that in Dari, we both got the idea of learning Dari while we were in Afghanistan. Happily for us, Aziz volunteered to be our teacher, and it was decided that we would meet every evening from Monday to Thursday for our lessons.

We began over a cup of tea or coffee. Aziz bought a primer, bright green in colour, which was used in the school system for five-year-olds. It had the Dari alphabet and pictures, in 20-font size. *Alif, bae, pae, tae, sae*, we went. Aleksandr, who is thirty-three years younger than me, was chattering away in Dari before too long, while I continued to be slow and tongue-tied. As much as Aziz and I tried, I just could not remember anything; I finally gave up on writing in Dari and concentrated solely on conversation. This suited me much better. I could now talk to the shopkeepers and children on the street, and began to understand when they asked me to come in for a cup of tea, or have an ice cream with them.

This also meant that I began to understand my students a little better. As the days went by, I started to understand what they were saying before it was translated. When a guest I had invited made a presentation in Dari, I understood at least 80 per cent of it. And when I made an effort to say something in Dari, the students smiled. I may not be able to write a novel or give a lecture in Dari, but it made me feel more connected to the place and its people.

Dari is a modern form of Persian used in administration,

government, radio, television, and print media in Afghanistan, as well as in parts of Iran and Tajikistan. In Afghanistan, it is the official language, along with Pashto. About 50 per cent of the Afghans and around 2.5 million people in Iran and Pakistan speak Dari as one of their primary languages.

Dari has contributed to the majority of Persian borrowings in other Asian languages, such as Urdu, Punjabi, Gujarati, etc. It was the administrative, official, cultural language of the Perso-centric Mughal Empire and served as the lingua franca throughout the South Asian subcontinent for centuries. The sizeable Persian component of the Anglo-Indian loan words in English and Urdu, therefore, reflects the Dari pronunciation. For instance, dopiaza or pyjama come from the Dari pronunciation, while in the Iranian Persian they're pronounced *do-piyāzeh* and *pey-jāmeh*. The Dari language has a rich and colourful tradition of proverbs that deeply reflect Afghan culture and relationships.

Violence in Kabul

While reports came in from several parts of the country about violence and destruction, I was cocooned in my guest house and life in Kabul and had felt relatively safe. This changed on the last day of a three-day hostile training course on how to survive in post-conflict Afghanistan. The first two days were spent in Kabul and the third day, at a shooting range, about 15 kilometres out of the city, on the road to the northern province of Jalalabad. By 10:30 a.m., we were at the range, and when we were ready to leave at around 1:00 p.m., we were told by the security company training us that the roads to Kabul were blocked off. We couldn't leave.

Several hours later, two security vehicles arrived from

Kabul and we were escorted back in a convoy that included an armoured vehicle. Windows up, doors locked, one car behind the other, we headed into the city. Initially, it seemed calm, but as we got closer to the centre we saw that the shop shutters were down, with only the naan and meat shops still open. The windows of the Kabul Serena were broken and two shops in the Kabul City Centre had been burnt.

We reached our office to find that our colleagues had stayed in the basement all day. There were bullets holes in the office boundary and the external walls of the office compound. Eventually, staff began to leave for home. We were informed that the offices and training centre were to remain closed the next day. Given a choice between either going home or staying, my students from the provinces decided to stay.

The atmosphere was uncertain and scary with an all-night curfew being declared. Two of my colleagues who lived in another part of Kabul stayed in our guest house, as their home was not safe. Calls were made to families and friends in France, USA, Pakistan, India and Belarus. Reports began to come in that several guest houses housing international staff were burnt, as was the office of the American NGO, Care.

The reason for all of this chaos was apparently an American convoy, coming south on the Jalalabad road during morning rush hour, that ran into several cars due to brake failure. The incident led to cars being crushed and many people getting injured. Local Afghans began to stone the convoy and the Americans, allegedly opened fire, killing several Afghans. This created a ripple through the city and led to incidents of rioting, arson and loot. Guns appeared from nowhere and young men appeared on camera shouting anti-American and anti-Karzai slogans.

Grieving for Afghanistan

I stayed home the day after the violence. It was a beautiful morning—crisp air, blue sky, and very sunny. As I sat in the garden with my morning tea and watched the birds and butterflies flying around the garden, chasing each other. I was grateful that they did not know or understand violence.

There was an uncomfortable silence about the night of rioting. A curfew was in place from 10:00 p.m. to 4:00 a.m. When Safi, the cook, came in on his bicycle, he informed us that things were now calm; there were armed forces on the streets and many police checkpoints. Shops were starting to open.

The phone started ringing at 7:30 a.m. Michael called to ask if I was safe and told me that our American-Afghan friend Yunus' guest house had been looted and burnt. When I immediately called Yunus to check if he was okay, he reassured me of his well-being and told me that he had slept in a safe place at night. Sigrid, the Australian from Brisbane, called to check if I had been able to establish contact with Grace, another Australian, whom she had not been able to get in touch with.

As my colleagues woke up I put on coffee, and made eggs and toast. Two Afghan colleagues dropped by to see if we were fine. One of them, who had travelled in a bus to get a feel of the local mood, said that there was a lot of anti-American sentiment being voiced.

Adele and Miriam went home briefly to collect essentials and to spend another night at the guest house. I advised Miriam against the idea of taking pictures in town. Trying to create some normality in such a tumultuous time, Adele and I made pasta with pesto, and a tomato and feta cheese salad. I also tried to do some work, but couldn't concentrate and was plagued by the feeling that I should be doing something different, not quite sure what.

I had a hard night with little or no sleep. I could hear Miriam on the phone next door, distressed. The guards across the street seemed to be talking louder than usual. I got up and shut the glass door to the terrace and could see planes and helicopters circling in the sky.

I woke up with a feeling of dread and extreme sadness—for a country that had just begun to see peace, a country where children had started to go to school, health centres were being built, and the economy was just picking up. But, for many, things were not moving fast enough. I wondered about the expectations that people had. Were they expecting that the American-led forces would leave, and the Afghans would now manage their country; that development would come faster; that there would be peace? Not being an Afghan and having never lived in an environment where there has been war and violence for 30 years, I do not quite know the answer to that, but I do know that I would be devastated.

When I see young men on the TV shouting "Death to Americans; Death to Karzai!" I know this is not the answer. They do it for the media, and the media laps it up. Without the American-led forces and President Karzai, would there be more or less violence in Afghanistan? The solution to the problem in Afghanistan is to create suitable conditions for the Afghans to take charge of their future, with some help from outside. I am aware that such an idea is immediately dismissed by those who think that Afghanistan is being treated as a playground for world forces, where big powers play out their geopolitical games. Perhaps, there are no easy answers.

But I am grieving—for Afghanistan and what went wrong

on Monday, May 30; for the lack of understanding between human beings; for us not giving each other the benefit of the doubt, for expecting the worst of each other and making it come true.

The calm after the storm

The fourth day after the rioting, looting, burning and destruction in Kabul was a Friday and Jumma.

There had been a great deal of speculation about what would happen on the first Friday after the riots. Curfew continued to be imposed and on Tuesday, most people stayed home, with schools and government offices also being asked to close. We returned to work on Wednesday, but one hour into my class, I was told to let the students go as the intelligence information suggested there could be demonstrations that might turn violent. All local staff was also sent home by noon.

Adele and I ventured out for a meeting at the UN complex. It was calm. On the last day of my two-week class, I asked the students what they thought had happened on Monday. They repeated what I had heard on the TV and through the local Afghans: the Americans were at fault, there was no brake failure, and they always behaved arrogantly on the roads with their convoys and SUVs, pushing aside traffic and pedestrians. Others said the American soldiers were drunk, and were dancing in their vehicles after they shot into the crowd of Afghans. The American version is that they were signalling to people and traffic to move out of the way, and had to shoot in the air to disperse the crowds that had started stoning and shooting at them.

While the truth was being sought, parliament was also in session, discussing the incident. The Americans in charge apologised, although quite weakly, and offered financial compensation to the families who had suffered losses. A commission was established both by parliament and the Americans to look into the incidents.

The UN and diplomatic community in Kabul are not allowed into many public places—markets, mosques, gardens, public transport, streets, restaurants, and homes that do not have sufficient security. At any sign of danger, they are "locked down", meaning that they are not allowed to leave their "compounds" or the secure areas in which they live. They miss out on interacting with Afghans and their hospitality, warmth and love. Consequently, the Afghans miss out on getting to know the diplomats as they are—human—just like themselves. This segregation has meant that they and their hosts (the Afghans) know little about each other, which only helps to perpetuate a climate of distrust.

This Friday, as the expatriates waited, hoping for no more trouble, the mullahs preached in the mosques. Aziz informed us that the parliamentarians had been in discussion with the mullahs all week, which explained the calm on the streets. A call for peace and healing was essential at the time. As was seeking the real reasons for the simmering discontent, the high unemployment, the high cost of living, and the perceived slow pace of development.

Healing a nation

A week later, and there continued to be little concrete information available. No matter who I asked about that fateful Monday, I heard the same stories about the "arrogant Americans", showing the glaring lack of trust between communities. Many did not even believe that the brakes of the convoy had failed. However, the feeling that dominated was one of general dissatisfaction with the nature and pace of development that had taken place since the Taliban were overthrown in 2001. Unemployment, especially in Kabul city, continued to be high, made worse by high inflation in housing and food prices. This fuelled the general perception that the international community's presence in the country was not needed.

Afghans feel and say that the presence of the UN, diplomatic community and NGOs has driven up the price of property, taken jobs from Afghans, and not delivered any tangible gains for them. The most common question is: what has happened to all the money that has come into the country as aid?

It is a good question. Afghanistan has been dependent on foreign aid due to its history and a lack of political cohesion in the country following the US-led operation in 2001. The economic situation is in part a result of the insecurity and instability that has created a "cause and effect" situation due to bad governance and high levels of corruption.

But it is not all doom and gloom. The economy and the security situation of Afghanistan have improved and, according to some analysts, the country is experiencing the most advanced, most democratic, most secure and most prosperous era in the last 35 years of its modern history.

An important factor in Afghanistan's economic recovery is the ever-increasing inflow of international aid and assistance. The growth of the service and agricultural sectors has also had a positive impact on the economy. However, living conditions of the Afghan people remain among the worst in the world. There is a lack of housing and shelter (especially in those areas with a higher number of internally displaced persons), medical care (in particular, maternal and child health), clean and safe water, public infrastructure are all lacking, and the crime rate continues to remain high.

There is also a deficit of skills and expertise in almost every sector. Non-Afghan companies, staff and techniques are being brought into the country to create infrastructure and systems. This is at all levels—from training parliamentarians to journalists, and building roads to schools. Afghans are naturally angry and resentful when they are told that they cannot manage their own country and need outside help for everything. There is an impatience to reap the benefits of development—something they haven't had for a long time—such as education, travel, jobs, money and physical comfort.

While development is vital to Afghanistan and will take time, there needs to be some form of healing to take place. There is sadness and anger about what has happened to their country among many Afghans; without any direction, these feelings have led to resentment against those in power and those with money.

Could international institutions working in Afghanistan introduce reconciliation and healing in their work? This may be done, for a start, by encouraging more mingling and dialogue between the expatriates, their organisations and Afghans. The print and electronic media can serve as ideal forums for such discussions and dialogue. They can also undertake to disseminate information on what is being done in Afghanistan, and the problems faced by different organizations and communities.

Development in Afghanistan is currently focused on taking care of the physical needs of people. But people and a nation also need spiritual care and healing. In Afghanistan, right now, nothing is more important than this.

The psychological fallout of violence

I have often wondered how Afghans have coped with the endless cycle of violence and uncertainty. Anna Badkhen of the Pulitzer Center, writes that in a war-wrecked country like Afghanistan the trademark symptoms of individual war trauma—depression, anguish, and hyper aggression—leave whole populations envenomed with sectarian and ethnic mistrust, and with the belief that only violence can end violence.

Badkhen says,

> Many Afghans have told me that they defied the 2006 government order to disarm and secretly kept their rifles stashed within easy reach—in shallow pits in their backyards, beneath the earthen floor of their houses, behind knotty poplar rafters holding up wattle-and-daub roofs. One taxi driver explained that his family owned enough rifles to arm an infantry squad. He kept a Luger Parabellum, wrapped in a camel-wool blanket, in his car. He said he felt threatened by government troops, police, Taliban, ethnic militias, and neighbours belonging to different ethnic groups—in short, by almost everybody who was not his kin.[12]

She goes on to say that in 2002, shortly after the Taliban government fell in Kabul, the U.S. Centers for Disease Control and Prevention dispatched a research team to Afghanistan to study the prevalence of mental trauma among civilians. Its nationwide survey remains the only modern, comprehensive inquiry into the mental health of Afghans. It found that 42 per cent of Afghans suffered from post-traumatic stress disorder and 68 per cent exhibited signs of major depression. In other words, up to 19 million of the country's roughly 25 million people were suffering from psychological injuries.

How does then this manifest in the day-to-day lives of Afghans?

footwear, kitchenware, frozen foods, cheeses, chocolates, dishes and travel gear. Many make it a point to stock up when in Dubai, and many others receive care packages through their embassy mail. Living in these conditions, with the constant security threat and limitations on movement, can often be stifling and seem quite unreal.

While the coming and going helps us get a break, it does make it difficult to maintain certain relationships with the country and the local people. Whenever I got really excited about some long-term ideas and work, I had to gently remind myself that I was only there for a short time.

A matter of nails

The air of Kabul is dry. When I moved here at the end of February, it was cold, dry, and dusty. Delhi is dry and dusty too, but not like Kabul. Within a week, my skin was looking and feeling like a crocodile's and I began to worry that my three-month supply of facial cream, moisturizer, and body oil would not last.

On March 8, to celebrate International Women's Day, I had dinner with my friend Federica at La Fontaine. Her German friend joined us. As we spoke about this and that, he remarked casually that this was the only country where even diplomats had dirt under their nails. I quickly looked at mine.

In Dari and Urdu, the word for nail is *nakhoon*—literally, without blood. So, while my nails were just dirty, it was the skin at the cuticles that was dry and cracked, and hurt every time it brushed against my scarf or paper. In Delhi, I had a manicure but it is expensive to get one in Kabul and I didn't have the patience or the implements to do one at home. Back in Delhi, I had a manicure done and it had never felt quite so special! It is amazing what you can get used to—after all, it is only a matter of nails.

In Delhi

I had been in Kabul for three months and it was time to take a break for two weeks in Delhi. Reaching the airport at 11:30 a.m., I was told that the flight was delayed by two hours. I checked-in and joined the ranks of waiting visitors in the lounge. As I waited with the others and chewed on the vegetarian submarine sandwiches and a Coke offered by the airline, I began talking to an American soil expert from Atlanta.

At 6:00 p.m., there was an announcement to say that the flight to Delhi was cancelled, and we were sent off to various hotels for the night. In my hotel group were hydro engineers from Nepal, journalists from a German TV network based in Delhi, the soil expert from Atlanta, Indian students studying medicine in Tajikistan, and a businessman operating cargo planes between Afghanistan, Tajikistan and India.

Over dinner and breakfast, we all got to know each other, and exchanged news and views about working in different countries. I invited my friends Shiraz (who was affiliated with the BBC) and Eberhard (associated with a German foundation) for breakfast at the hotel we were housed in, overlooking the hill that the novel and film *The Kite Runner* was shot in. After the omelettes, toast and coffee, I introduced Eberhard to the German TV crew and they exchanged story ideas.

I got to Delhi a full twenty-four hours later than I was supposed to. In this time, I got to know people I would not normally have met or talked to, or eaten and shared experiences with. I stayed at a hotel I had not heard of, and felt enriched by the twenty-four hours in unexpected ways.

As I was about to leave on June 15, the *Guardian* reported that an American-led force of 11,000 troops had launched the biggest anti-Taliban offensive in Afghanistan since 2001, concentrating their fire-power on an area under British control. The ambitious offensive, named Operation Mountain Thrust, aimed to cripple the increasing insurgency before NATO took command of southern Afghanistan in August.

The heaviest combat was expected in the mountains spanning western Uruzgan province and north-eastern Helmand, where 3,300 British troops were deployed, and Britain had suffered its first combat fatality the past weekend. Less intensive operations would target pockets of Kandahar and Zabul provinces. US military officials announcing the operation said reconstruction activities would follow in its wake.

"This is not just about killing or capturing extremists," said US spokesman Tom Collins in Kabul. "We are going to go into these areas, take out the security threat and establish conditions where government forces, government institutions [and] humanitarian organisations can move in and begin the real work." British troops would fight alongside 2,300 Americans, 2,200 Canadians and about 3,500 Afghans. The mission was to last through the summer and carried a high risk of casualties.

Dilbar Jan Arman, the governor of Zabul, one of the four targeted provinces, said US forces and local leaders had been planning the operation for the past two months. "We will search for the Taliban wherever they are. We seek to disrupt their underground networks. We hope it will be a success," he told the *Guardian* in the provincial capital, Qalat.

This multinational operation was the broadest and most ambitious strike against the Taliban after 2001. Benjamin Freakley, the US major-general commanding operations in

Afghanistan, said the troops would target Taliban hideouts across the four provinces.

"They'll be in one area, they'll move out of that area, they'll conduct an attack in another area, and then move back to a safe haven," he told the Associated Press. "This is our approach to put simultaneous pressure on the enemy's networks, to cause their leaders to make mistakes, and to attack those leaders."

A kilim is forever

I love kilims. Whenever I see one I like, I feel excited, get goose pimples, and am tempted to own it immediately. In my travels I have collected kilims from Tunisia, Turkey, Iran, Pakistan and Afghanistan. There are many countries where kilims are produced, and their designs and colours are influenced by their area of production. Kilims are different from carpets, consisting of a flat weave of weft and warp. Unlike carpets, they have no pile. They feel different under your feet. Not as luxurious as carpets, where the pile reaches to meet the sole of your foot.

Kilim making, along with Islam, spread through the Near East, Middle East, and Central Asia, via invading armies and traders. Tribal people used carpets and kilims as floor coverings, saddle-bags, horse blankets, and even as bands on round nomadic tents (*yurts*), or as door flaps. They have a beauty of their own and come in all sizes, depending on the size of the loom. Nomadic tribes would often weave on a loom small enough to be easily transported, and would therefore produce narrower carpets or kilims than those made on the larger village-based looms.

On my third day in Kabul in March, Aleksandr and I walked into the Herat Carpet Centre and met Wahid Abdullah, the owner. Tall, with an open face and calm demeanour, I warmed to Wahid instantly. This chemistry is important in a kilim transaction, as in any transaction, for that matter. We looked at kilims and asked him to put three aside, as I did not have the cash and there was no credit card transaction in Afghanistan yet. I went back, bought them, and in my reorganized room at the guest house, they provided immediate warmth and colour.

I spoke passionately about my kilims to my friends in the UN and diplomatic community, who are not allowed to roam on Chicken Street, where most of the kilim shops are. Brenda and Marie did not even know what they were. Marie wanted some and I said I would get them, my heart pounding with excitement at the idea of going back to Wahid's shop. They trusted my choice, they said. I bought three for Marie.

Soon, Brenda wanted some. I was back at Wahid's and got her three, different from Marie's, but regionally varied—one Baluchi, one Tatar and an Uzbeki. I also took Diane, my friend visiting from New York, to Wahid's shop. Diane too is a kilim and carpet-lover. We spent two hours in Wahid's 6 x 4' shop. As we dismantled his shop, the colours, designs and varieties leapt out at us. Diane—a more discerning buyer—wanted to know how old the kilims were, checked them thoroughly, and decided on five. The two more expensive ones she set aside, to be looked at in the daylight.

I, on the other hand, trust my intuition completely. Do I like the colour, design and the way I think it will fit in my home? I have to fall in love with it, want it badly. It is like choosing crystal—look for the one that is looking for you.

Buying a kilim you will love means suspending judgement—on quality, age, and value for money. I am happy to do all this, feel the rush, and fall in love. A kilim, like a diamond, is forever. Only, I prefer kilims to diamonds.

Found in translation

In class, I asked the students to describe the most important lesson from the field trip of the day before. Half-way through the class, while Fanoos translated back and forth, a rather animated discussion broke out.

Let me explain. I teach in English. Fanoos translates into Dari, and sometimes Pashto, the other language predominantly spoken in Afghanistan. He then translates back into English for me. This time there are at least 7 (out of 14) students whose first language is Pashto. A Dari speaker complained about the Pashto speakers wanting translation. I was a little taken aback, and said we would take as much time as was needed to translate from any one language to another. In the midst of this entire hullabaloo, one student put up his hand and said neither Dari nor Pashto suited him as his first language was Uzbeki!

Fanoos asked him to share his experience in Uzbeki. When the student was done, he translated what he had said into Dari. All the students clapped for him. I explained how we could use language as a challenge, rather than a liability. Here, I was an English speaker, listening to them in Dari. I was studying it, and was pleased with myself as I understood more and more, with each day and each class. And the students' English improved, as they asked me to spell out words and made a note of them. Nothing gives me more pleasure than to hear them say, "Please teacher, what is the meaning of....?"

Some students, knowing more English than the others, try to speak in English. I can see the other students look on in disapproval, and I ask them to speak in Dari instead.

About 35 per cent of Afghans are Pashto speaking, and 50 per cent speak Afghan Persian or Dari. Most Afghans are bilingual. In Kabul, Dari is more widely spoken, with the change of regime from the Pashto-speaking Taliban to the Dari-speaking Northern Alliance. Other languages are Turkic, Uzbek and Turkmen (about 11 per cent).

A great deal has been written about being lost in translation, but for me, a great deal can be found in translation.

Gifts of love

Yesterday, as I was going up the stairs to my first floor office at the training centre, a student from my reproductive health class stopped me in the corridor. He held out two mini-sized muskmelons. For you and your friend (Diane), he said.

Is it from Helmand, I asked? Yes, he said. I was touched. *Tashakor,* I said, putting my right hand to my heart. I love this gesture, one which people in Afghanistan make all the time. I smiled all the way up the stairs.

Returning home, I stopped at the naan shop and picked one for lunch. The man at the shop wouldn't take money for it. At home, Diane and I prepared lunch. I cut the two melons, thinking about the 38-year old student from Helmand, father of seven children. He has a fierce shock of very black hair, a moustache and beard. His eyes, when they lock into mine, do not turn away. I smile, he smiles. The melon, which Diane and I ate with naan, cheese, hummus, tomatoes and mango juice, tasted ever so special.

On the final day of my last reproductive health class, evaluations were filled out, cookies and soda passed around in celebration, and certificates handed out. One of the students brought a friend who played the guitar and sang. A poem expressing appreciation for me was read out, and later handed to me, signed by all the students. I asked my colleague Omar to translate it from Dari to English, so I could understand and cherish it.

They thanked me for leaving my home and relatives and coming to Afghanistan to serve the new generation of journalists. They said they didn't have the words to express appreciation, but that I had a special place in their hearts. They hoped I wouldn't forget them.

But the greatest gift from my students is their openness in discussing very personal and difficult issues in class. Issues, which are taboo in their culture—sex, marriage, love, passion, relationships between women and men, violence and abuse, HIV/AIDS—and much more.

I love the way they call me 'teacher' and Ustad; the way they ask for permission to come into class if they are late; how they stand when I come in class; and how when class ends they want me to leave the room first. These are all gifts of love, tangible and intangible, and they make my day, every day.

A change of pace

My normally slow pace of existence in Kabul changed when my friend Diane came to visit. We had worked together in India in the mid-90s, and she now lives in New York. Diane is the only person who offered to visit me in Kabul; but I also hesitated to invite people, not sure how they would respond to my life in Afghanistan.

Since Diane is here, we have been up at 6:30 a.m. (sometimes, even earlier). To spend more time with Diane, I asked for my two classes to be scheduled back to back. While I took my classes in the morning, Diane used my desk to work on her assignments, as my colleagues took care of her. After classes, we would head home, pick up a naan from the shop on the way, and make lunch. We kept it light as it was fairly hot and we had a lot to do.

Nuristani box

After lunch, we would venture out to our favourite Chicken Street. For hours, Diane and I poured over rings, kilims, trying on chapans, and lusting over Nuristani furniture (from the northern province of Nuristan).

We took a side trip to the Kabul Museum, now rebuilt after almost total destruction. The Darulaman Palace, next to the museum, is in disrepair, bombed and broken, but it is still possible to see the grandeur of the Palace. We walked around Babur's tomb and garden, which was also being renovated.

On Saturday we drove north to Shamali and Istalif and came away with the most exquisite pottery, to eat out of or perhaps just look at and admire. We lunched at Polisayad in Kappisa Province where the rivers Panjsheer, Solang and Shitur meet.

Aziz, our driver, took his first-ever horse ride through the waters. In a restaurant on the water, we spread out on floor

Nuristani cupboard

mats and cushions covered with bright velvet covers, and ate fish, rice and naan. We downed this with *dogha*, a drink made of yogurt, cucumber, and spices. Every now and then we looked up at the marvellous scenery, water meeting land, land meeting mountains, and mountains meeting the sky, through the pink and red geraniums in planters hanging over the railings. It was a hot and dusty trip, but very memorable.

Diane came to my reproductive health class and joined us on a trip to the Nejat Centre, a drug rehab NGO. She met my other expat friends for brunch at the Kabul Serena and also on the night of BBQ and live music at the Canadian compound. We sat out in the guest house garden every day, looking at the butterflies' chase each other, the sun setting, and felt the cool breeze at night as we gazed up at the bright stars.

As Diane flew out, I was taking my class to the Mir Bacha Kot health clinic. The pace of my life already felt slow without her.

Men, women and reproduction

Yesterday, in my reproductive health class, the topic was HIV and AIDS and male responsibility. The students were very interested in learning about HIV and AIDS. In a class of twelve, three were women. In a segregated society, such as Afghanistan, it is difficult for them to feel comfortable in a room where sex and sexuality (which is at the heart of reproductive health) is being discussed, and I had to work hard to devise different ways to present the topics.

This is my third reproductive health class, so I have some experience of how the students react. In my previous class, I had a young fourteen-year-old woman who spent the better part of class with her head lowered. Women in the class tend to mostly sit together. However, by the third or fourth day of the classes, there was a fair amount of camaraderie between them.

While discussing male responsibility, I said men make good advocates for reproductive health as they have more power in society and over sexual relations. I asked who all agreed with this and only two men felt otherwise. When I asked them to elaborate, the older married student said women have more power as they often refuse sex to men, and if they agreed, they asked for favours—in money and jewellery. The younger single student said men spent a lot of time thinking about women and loving them, while women didn't care that much, and had the power to make men fall in love with them! There was a great deal of laughter over these remarks.

I talked about the socialisation of women and how women learn to manipulate, often from watching their mothers; how women feel inadequate and less powerful in relationships; how they did what they could to negotiate for a better status. I talked about the need for equality in relationships.

I said that men had the power to initiate contraception in relationships, use condoms to prevent sexually transmitted diseases, and support women during pregnancy and childbirth. I also said that they could create an environment in their homes where boys would learn to love and respect women, so they could be good partners when they grew up.

I decided to focus on what they had found particularly difficult in a previous session—speaking to children about sex, at home or otherwise. At the beginning of the class, Abdul from Helmand, father of seven children, said that contraception should not be discussed with young people as it would encourage them to have sex, but by the end of the class he had reversed his position. The students told me it was the best class they had attended, and my heart lifted.

Mending Afghanistan, stitch by stitch

She's American, he's Afghan. They met in 1979 in Tajikistan, where she was studying linguistics and he was studying engineering. She returned to America, got married, had children and worked in textiles and graphic design. He returned to Afghanistan, a land plagued by war and destruction. She's Charlotte. He's Sakhi.

In 1998, when the Taliban took over, Sakhi moved to Pakistan as a refugee. He located Charlotte through an Internet search, asking her to come to Pakistan and help the women of his community. She came to Lahore, and they started a project with the women doing one of the things they knew best—sewing and embroidery. And, Rubia, the organisation, was born.

In 2001, after 9/11 and the fall of the Taliban, Charlotte and Sakhi came to Afghanistan. Now, Rubia is registered as an Afghan business with a support group in the US and Europe. Almost 300 women have been trained to develop their skills and run the business. They work in their homes, between chores, making bags, shawls; cushion, cell phones, iPad and water-bottle covers. The embroidery is local and traditional, and carries a social message.

In a land over run by opium cultivation, trafficking and rampant drug use, *Sew, do not Grow,* is the message in Dari. The personal becomes political, and the political becomes personal. Another cushion cover has a traditional Uzbeki design, which is also the Rubia logo—the reds, greens, blues, maroons and mustards—all blend together in perfect harmony.

I first met Charlotte and was introduced to Rubia products when Diane and I were at the Serena Hotel. As we were leaving, Charlotte gave me her business card which said *Rubia,*

Mending Afghanistan, Stitch by Stitch, under the logo. I really liked the idea of Rubia, the logo, Charlotte and their products and decided I wanted to interview her at a later date.

I meet Charlotte, Sakhi and a helper at the end of a garden sale in one of Kabul's guest houses. The sun is low in the sky. I turn on my tape recorder and talk to Charlotte in English, and to Sakhi in Hindi, Urdu and Punjabi. We drink mineral water and Sakhi lights a cigarette. I ask them how they met. Charlotte laughs and says, ask Sakhi. He starts by telling me about their first meeting in Tajikistan, how he came back to his country which was devastated by war and conflict, his move to Pakistan and the condition of women in the refugee camps. I wanted to do something, he said, but I was a man. So, I thought about Charlotte and felt she could help me.

Charlotte chips in with her version of what she found when she reached Peshawar. Women were emotionally fragile, without any education and skills to make a living. What they could do, however, was embroider. It took a while to build their trust. "I was patient," says Charlotte, "and Sakhi was there to guide and help me." Slowly, the project got off the ground, women now had a money-making venture and this evolved into adult literacy classes for them. Younger women and girls began to flock to the project and classes, and a community developed.

After the fall of the Taliban, says Sakhi, the move back to Afghanistan was equally difficult. While the women were happy to be back in their own land, there were challenges. They had to rebuild their lives. Over time, the project got a new lease of life and went from success to success.

Charlotte and Sakhi are examples of many such collaborative ventures between Afghans and non-Afghans. Afghans who left the country as students and refugees had an opportunity to

Rubia cushion cover with poppy flower

see and experience other cultures and ways of working, and are now back to help rebuild the country.

Tomorrow, Sakhi and Charlotte are off to the US and Santa Fe, for the international Folk Art Festival, where they will hold a workshop and show their products. Then, it is a month in New Hampshire—where there are more shows and workshops. They will travel with Hafisa, one of their star workers.

They get ready to leave. All the products are packed in two large duffel bags by the helper. There are business cards to be printed at the shop around the corner. Charlotte picks up her sling bag stuffed with—among other things—her laptop. "This is my travelling office," she says, laughing, her blue eyes twinkling. In the countryside, she has a solar battery pack to charge her laptop.

They make quite a pair: he, tall with a face full of history, in a white salwar kameeze and black waistcoat, and she in her pink top with beige slacks and sneakers. Both mending Afghanistan, stitch by stitch.

The naan shop

It is July. I wake up at 6:45 a.m. as I have a date with the naan makers on my street, the shop I pass by every day. Mahmood, the one Hindi/Urdu speaking naan maker, invited me when I told him I wanted to watch the process of making naans and take photographs. For the last four months, I have seen Mahmood and two men almost every day. They call out to me when I pass by and ask if I am well. We say Salaam to each other, and I often buy a naan.

My naan shop, as I like to think of it, starts its work at 5:30 in the morning. It is a 6 x 4′ construction on the road. It has an open facade, from which clients access the shop and naans;

a side entrance to allow them to come and go, and an opening in the ceiling to let the smoke out. There is a deep pit in the middle of the floor, in which wooden sticks are embedded for the fire. The walls are covered with soot.

The three men work together. One kneads the whole-wheat flour patties with his hands, and then stamps them with a wooden spiked gadget—which makes little holes in the naan. The second man places the naan on a rectangular board covered with a cloth, firms it down, and slaps it into the pit. The third keeps the fire going and removes the naans with a six-foot thin metal rod. To avoid the naans from getting too dry, they sprinkle water into the pit.

Every now and then they wipe the sweat off their faces with their shirts. There is a large green floor fan but there is no electricity this morning. Everything is really still in the shop.

I watch the process silently, not wanting to distract them. I have many questions, but they can wait. Customers come and go, scooping up armfuls of the regular naan. A special roghan naan is being made for me—with ghee. But it does not stop there. Today, they put almonds in it. I watch all this, feeling very special. The naan is then put into the pit, cooked, and brought out with great love. A child helper is dispatched to bring a sheet of paper, and the naan is wrapped in it. It is really hot!

I hold out a ten Afghani note. They will not take it. We argue back and forth and, frustrated, I tuck the note away. Clutching the naan like a precious child, I leave, thanking them and waving goodbye.

Back home, I make spice tea with milk and sugar, put cheese and honey on the naan, rinse out some raisins and walnuts, and my breakfast is ready. As I write this, I have to stop and wipe the honey off my fingers.

Recipe for Naan

Traditional naan is made using a starter (*khamir toursh*), but this recipe uses packet yeast. The secret is a super-hot oven and the right amount of humidity.

5 cups regular flour
2 tsp kosher salt
1 packet quick rising yeast
5 tsp vegetable oil
2 cups warm water
1 tsp black sesame seeds (optional)
1 spray bottle filled with water

Put the flour, salt and yeast in the bowl of a food processor fitted with a dough blade. Process it for a few seconds to mix the ingredients. Continue to process as you dribble the oil into the flour. Next, slowly add the water to the flour with the processor running. If the mixture sticks to the sides of the processor, scrape it down and process some more. After a few minutes, the dough will come together in one smooth lump and it will move around the food processor. Let it swirl a couple of times and then it is ready to rest.

The naan shop

If you do not have a food processor, you can make the bread by hand. Pour all the dry ingredients in a big bowl and mix well. Add oil and mix further. Gradually add the water and knead the dough for 10 to 15 minutes till the dough is smooth and elastic. Once the dough is done, set it in a large bowl, cover with two dishcloths and keep in a warm place for two hours. Punch down the dough. It is ready to be baked.

Pre-heat oven to 500° F. Cover a large baking sheet with aluminium foil and set in the oven to heat. Spread some flour on the work surface and pat your hands with flour to keep the dough from sticking to your hands. Divide the dough into three balls and work it gently into an oval that measures about 1.5 ft. long and half an inch thick. As you stretch the dough it will pick up some of the flour from the work surface, make sure that you add more flour or the dough will stick to the work surface. Once the dough is shaped, make three deep lines lengthwise (do not cut the dough) on the surface of the dough with a knife.

When the oven is very hot, remove the baking sheet. Gently lay the shaped dough onto the baking pan and sprinkle with sesame seeds. Gently press the seeds into the dough. Place the dough in the oven, spray five to six times, and bake for five minutes. After five minutes, spray the bread five to six times, and continue to bake for another five minutes. The naan should be golden brown and crusty on the outside.

To keep the bread moist, wrap the warm bread in a large dishcloth until it cools down. Be sure to taste it while it is still warm. Cut in into three inch squares. Store in a Ziploc bag and place in the fridge. Reheat it in the toaster oven and enjoy it with feta cheese and a dab of cherry jam along with a cup of tea. I found this recipe in *www.afghancooking.net.*

The two week countdown

Two weeks from today, I will be on a flight to Delhi. The countdown has begun and I find myself caught between my worlds in Kabul and Delhi. Every day, it is the last of something, at least for this round.

Sunday was the first day of my last class. As I distributed the student information forms and listened to the students introduce themselves, I thought this is the last time I will be doing this. When I introduced myself, I had a hard time focusing. Today, we had a field trip to the Counter Narcotics Police of Afghanistan's office for a briefing. It was my fourth and last time.

I look out of my window and see the orange blooms on the pomegranate tree. The bright red fruit has begun to appear and bobs up and down in the early evening breeze. The grapes on the vines get bigger, slowly. I didn't realise they took so long, not ever having been so close to them. An old man came to cut the grass over the weekend. I won't see him again.

Coming home from work today, I stopped by the shop to buy milk. Found fresh spinach and lemons. The naan maker came into the shop and asked if I cooked for myself. Yes, I said. Why, he asked, does the cook not make your meals—Afghan food? I hesitate. He does, I say, but I like to cook and he uses too much oil. We both laugh. I promise to bring halwa on Friday. Sure, he says, his hand to his heart.

Back home, Faiz, the guard, lets me in. He has been told that he will not be required as of August. The shared house is being shut down and given up. He, Sabur, Safi, the other guards, and Fatima, the cleaner, will all be looking for other jobs. I am sad for them. It is a strange feeling. I'm having a hard time. Every now and then, I am a little tearful.

Leonard Cohen

I often buy music the way I buy wine or a book—by its cover. So it was with Leonard Cohen. About four years ago, at a music shop in Khan Market in Delhi, I found Cohen's Ten New Songs in my hands. I went home and played it, again, and again, and again. Sitting in Kabul, as I write this, I am still playing it. Cohen's deep voice is highly seductive. Sharon

Robinson, a backup singer, shares all the songs with him. They harmonise beautifully together.

Late last year, I bought a book by one of my favourite travel writers—Pico Iyer. What do I find when I open the book? The first essay is on Leonard Cohen. How is this possible, I thought? I was delighted.

Cohen's music is haunting, intense, focusing on love, beauty and despair. It has a wonderful Zen-like quality to it, deeply meditative, and stays with you for a long time. All ten numbers on the CD are different yet similar, set apart by the lyrics, but joined together by their ability to connect with one's innermost feelings.

Back on Boogie Street

A sip of wine, a cigarette, and then it is time to go,
I've tidied up the kitchenette; I tuned the old banjo
So come, my friend
Be not afraid
We are so lightly here
It is in love that we are made
And in love we disappear

In my secret life

I saw you this morning
You were moving so fast
Can't seem to loosen my grip
Down the path
And I miss you much
There is no one in sight
And we are still making love
In my secret life, in my secret life

I smile when I am angry, I cheat and I lie
I do what I have to do
To get by
But I know what is wrong and I know what is right
And I die for the truth
In my secret life, in my secret life

I think about our lives and secrets—how little we know of ourselves and other people. If I do not share something of myself with others, is it a secret? Do secrets help or hurt us? Or, as Leonard says:

> In my secret life, in my secret life
> I smile when I am angry, I cheat and I lie
> I do what I have to do
> To get by
> But I know what is wrong and I know what is right
> And I die for the truth

A wedding

When Najiba, the 21-year old Afghan woman, came to work as the assistant gender and human rights trainer, I didn't expect it to be such a short stay.

Two weeks after she joined, I asked her what she thought about marriage. I am not interested, she said rather vehemently, adding that her younger sister was already married with a child. I asked her what her family thought about her lack of interest in marriage. She said her mother supported her but her father wasn't sure.

I watched her as she slipped into her role. She had the presence that was needed for a trainer. She stood tall, her slim body dressed in Afghan style—pants or skirts, with long tops, a jacket and a headscarf or shawl. She had a strong voice that woke students up, should they be inclined to have a quick nap during a discussion on male domination or violence against women. A nice smile, and a keen sense of humour.

After my two week break in Delhi, imagine my surprise when she asked me to help her in negotiating with the management to work half-time. "Why?" I asked. "Because I am getting married," she said.

She said her parents had introduced her to a young man whom she liked. It was that simple. As she told me this, Najiba was rather fetchingly dressed in a bright green skirt and a tight, top-hugging green blouse. I smiled, swallowing my disappointment, and said that I would help her.

"How much time do you need off and will you be coming back to work after the wedding?" I asked her.

"Yes, of course. Everyone in his family works and I told them I would not stop working," she said.

"How about your husband?" I asked.

"Well, he does not want me to work and said that I don't need to work. He says he will give me double the amount of money that I get here."

"Do not make that mistake, don't stop working. It is not good for you or your relationship," I tell her.

Najiba started leaving at noon every day, after the morning class. She was on the phone a lot, pacing up and down, gesturing. She was distracted and irritable. Hey, I told her, you are supposed to be happy. I'm stressed out, she said. I smiled. Then, one day, she was gone. Her wedding card arrived—cream background with grey, silver and gold embossed flowers and a scalloped edging. The date was July 7.

The insert was an invitation in Dari. I asked Omar to translate it for me. It started with a prayer to both worlds—

heaven and hell. It went on to say that spring was beautiful with flowers in the sun; the night was beautiful with stars in the sky; and the wedding party was beautiful with me as a guest. The two families invited me to the wedding ceremony of the couple.

The reception was at 5:00 p.m., at the 1001 Nights Wedding Hall in Khairkhana. The management of the hotel requested that there be no children or cameras. My colleague Omar translated all this, and I wrote it down. It was my first Afghan wedding card.

Not everyone in the office had been invited. Those who were, discussed the wedding gift. Salim turned around, with a thoughtful look on his face, stretched out his arms and said, how about a big TV? Adele and I looked at each other. Everyone has a TV, I said. Besides, shouldn't we find out if Najiba is going to live with her husband's family, or will they have their own apartment and a TV? Who will know? Soraya, we all said together. She was Najiba's friend and they shared an office and often had lunch together, heads bent over their lunch boxes.

I go looking for Soraya, who is squinting at the computer screen. Do you know if Najiba is going to live with her husband's family? Yes, says Soraya. Is she going to live in an apartment with her husband? Yes, says Soraya. I give up. As it turns out, Soraya has not been invited (somebody could have told me).

Back in the room, Adele and I start talking about gifts we would give—Istalif pottery, kilims, and Nuristani boxes. Our Afghan colleagues ignore us and carry on like we are not there.

Next day, the discussion continues. Omar walks into our office and I ask him—what should we give Najiba? He sits down, crosses his right leg over his left knee, and says: a washing machine. Adele flares up. Pressure cookers, washing machines—is this what she will do with her life? Omar is startled. I laugh. Yes, all women wash clothes, and even her husband can operate the machine, says Omar. Sure, says Adele!

It is very unromantic, I say, to no one in particular. Gadgets as wedding gifts are unromantic, I repeat for emphasis. Omar looks at me. Adele is not giving up. How about a rice cooker she asks, banging on her laptop keys. Omar's eyes light up. Yes, he says, and two sacks of rice. A goat, I say. For meat curry and rice. We laugh hysterically.

Adele says a washing machine is too expensive—40,000 Afs. Omar describes the last gift he and a group of friends organised—a set of plates and two beautiful platters. Good idea, Adele and I say. Omar is despatched to collect 250 Afs (US $5) from those who will give it. The money is given to me. You buy the gift, says Omar.

I learn that the gift is not given on the day of the wedding. We have to visit the couple in their new home and give the gift then. That will be next week. The discussion goes back to who all are going to the wedding, what time, and how.

It is the day of the wedding. It is agreed, by all those who are going, that we will reach the marriage hall by 7:00 p.m. Dinner, I asked? From my experience of Indian weddings, I felt we may want to give it a miss. Maybe we could eat out, I suggest to the group that is going. No answer.

At 5:45 p.m., Adele, her brother, Mathew, who is visiting, and I head to my guest house to shower and change. The plan was for Aziz to pick us up by 6:30 p.m., and we would swing by Adele's place where she and Mathew would change for the wedding and we would be at the marriage hall by 7:00 p.m.

But Aziz got confused about the plans and came late. So, Adele and Mathew ended up wearing whatever they could find in my wardrobe. At the hall, Mathew was sent off with the guys to the men's section, and Adele and I went to the women's section—four flights up. In some weddings, the male and female guests can sit together but that was not the case here.

The hall was huge, full of women and children. I looked for a table—and spotted one in the left corner of the hall. As we got there, Adele said, where is Najiba? We retraced our steps and there, on the podium and sofa, sat Najiba and her new husband. Should we come, I gesture? Yes, yes, she said. The photographer was summoned; we were introduced to her husband, and pictures taken. I asked the photographer to take pictures with my camera as well. He obliged.

Najiba was dressed in a sea green outfit with a veil, a tiara at the side of her head, hair swept up. Her make-up was very white and she had long false eyelashes, and lots of shiny stuff all over. Her husband wore a tie and a suit. We moved away from the podium, and sat at a closer table. About 15 minutes later, the young couple left the hall.

The hall was decorated with white and green banners and plastic flowers. A four-person band was playing music, mostly Hindi songs, as women and children danced. Others sat at round tables, with white tablecloths. A tray of sugared almonds was offered to us.

By 10:00 p.m., we were starving and called the guys. They were eating. The music was loud; Adele and I could barely hear ourselves talking and we had been discovered by the children, who got under the table and were pulling at Adele's skirt. Having taken the obligatory photos, it was time to go. Adele and I came down the four flights of stairs to the parking space. The moon was spectacular, the stars were bright and there was a gentle breeze. We sat in the garden and waited for the guys. I asked Omar where the marriage ceremony would take place. In another room with family, much later, he said. We left, stopped at a kebab place to eat, as Adele and I had not eaten. Omar suggested a place with local music and off we went.

The gift for Najiba

I finally found a gift for Najiba after a long search. On a Friday, I asked Aziz to take me to the Parisian Store where there was a choice of crockery, cutlery, aluminium, plastic and ceramic (besides canned and dried food).

I first looked at the ceramic but didn't like the designs. Then there was the melamine crockery. I liked the design, but not the melamine. I loved the plastic trays, but I stopped myself—not romantic enough. Aziz took me to another store—in the basement and quite fancy. Shiny cups and saucers, watches, knives and forks sets. Nothing for us here, I thought. We left. I called Miriam for advice and Aziz called his father. Both suggested we go to the large open-air market near the canal. Aziz and I looked at each other—it was hot so we decided against going there.

"Let's try the Kabul City Centre," suggested Aziz. The Kabul City Centre is the new sparkling shopping centre in the middle of town. There is one glass and ceramic store here on the second floor, the guard said. It was a small shop, but with many interesting possible wedding gifts. Whatever I touched was too expensive—lemonade set, three times our budget. Six glasses, Italian, much below the budget. A jug to match, I asked. No, said the shopkeeper.

Bending down towards the glass case, I spotted glasses with a gold band of delicate work. What about these? I asked. From the Czech Republic, he said. Yes, yes, yes. I chose six, all within the budget. They were beautiful. "Aziz, if I gave you these for your wedding, would you like them?" I asked. Yes, he blushed fetchingly. Next day, when I took the gift into the office, there was appreciation and approval.

Nejat—rehabilitating drug addicts

Travelling south on Darulaman Street towards Parliament is the well-known Habibia High School. Destroyed during the Taliban years, it was rebuilt with assistance from the Indian government.

If you take a left at the school and go down the road, you get to the Nejat Centre, an Afghan NGO working on drug de-addiction. Upon entering, the first thing you see is the garden. Roses are in bloom. To the right is a reception room and behind it, about twenty men sit around under a canopy that keeps the sun out. It is 42°C and really hot.

The seventeen students in my drugs class are ushered into the large meeting room, and I go to greet the Director, Dr. Tariq Suliman. After exchanging pleasantries, we go to the hall where the staff from the centre and the students are already in discussion. Dr Suliman and his colleagues tell us about the Centre, the addicts who come to them and the challenges they face. The briefing complete, we go up the stairs to the rooms that are dedicated to the twenty men here for the fourteen-day de-addiction programme. The Centre does not have the space to accommodate more addicts or to keep them here for longer periods of time. There is a great demand for this programme.

A 2010 United Nations Office of Drug Control survey showed that around one million Afghans between the ages of 15 to 64 were addicted to drugs. At eight per cent of the population, this rate was twice the global average. Providing drug treatment to users is essential, but an estimated 700,000 Afghans have no access to treatment. Centres were operational across a mere 21 of the 34 provinces and could only provide treatment to some 10,000 drug users a year. Nejat Centre is only one such scarce facility in Afghanistan.

The men sitting in discussion under the canopy are outpatients. They come to the centre at 9:00 a.m. and leave at 3:30 p.m. During this time, they receive counselling, talk to each other, have lunch together, do exercises and yoga, sing and play musical instruments.

There is a community programme for women, as it is taboo for them to be seen in a place like Nejat. And, says Dr. Suliman, the families will not even admit that women (and girl children) have a drug problem. Tomorrow, two women students in the class will accompany the women staff of Nejat to visit the women addicts in their homes.

In 1991, Dr. Suliman and several of his medical school colleagues fled to Pakistan. There he witnessed the death of a young man, a drug addict, who was a relative of a doctor in their group. Suliman and his colleagues, shocked at this state of affairs and their ignorance of drug use among Afghans, set up Nejat.

In 2002, Dr. Suliman and his colleagues returned to Afghanistan, and brought Nejat with them. Since then, the Centre has initiated several programmes—drug reduction, de-addiction, rehabilitation, income generation and awareness. They have programmes on HIV and AIDS, and special programmes with NGOs working with street children who are particularly vulnerable to sexual abuse and addiction.

Using traditional Afghan concepts such as the Hujra (hospitality room) as well as a group interaction programme called Dosti (friendship), Nejat has a very down-to-earth approach to dealing with addicts. The core philosophy of its therapy is love and compassion. This is very evident, and you feel it in when you are among them. The staff is well trained; there is no judgement, disapproval or blame.

The participants in the two-week residential programme are dressed in black and their heads are shaved. This gives them a somewhat uniform look. They are in various stages of de-addiction. Some are more bright-eyed and alert than others. They are eager to talk to the students, who are often afraid. I nudge them gently towards the addicts. Go and talk to them, I say. I lead by example, wishing the addicts, shaking hands with them, and introducing myself.

On the walls, above their beds, is a writing wall, where they are encouraged to express themselves. There are drawings and poetry about love, hope and regret.

The Centre has an annual budget of US $30,000. Like everything in Afghanistan, they can use more funds and more long-term support than just year-to-year funding, but Dr. Suliman takes all this in his stride.

Soul cooking

In Kabul, I have been cooking more than I do back in Delhi. While there is a cook who cooks for all of us, I prefer slightly lighter food, so have opted out of group eating. I make food that is quick to prepare, good to taste, pleasant to look at, and nourishing for my health and that of my friends.

I prefer fresh ingredients, as the food tastes better, a calm environment to cook in and attractive and appropriate serving dishes that complement the cooking. These are my two most often cooked dishes.

Nuts over rice

Do you like rice? Want to serve it to yourself and your guests in a special way? Since coming to Afghanistan, where nuts are plenty, I have begun to use this recipe quite a bit. I serve it with spinach, dhal, yogurt, and chutney. This dish also keeps well. I refrigerate it, heat it gently with a sprinkle of water the next day, and take it to work to share with my colleagues.

Ingredients (4 servings)

1½ cups rice (white or brown is fine)
3 cups water
1 tbsp olive oil
Handful of almonds, raisins and walnuts
2 tbsp butter

Put the rice and water in a pot. Cook till the rice is done.

Sliver the almonds, wash the raisins, and break the walnuts into small pieces. Heat the olive oil in a pan and sauté the nuts for about three minutes.

When the rice is done, put two tbsp of butter, add the nuts, and stir gently. Cover with a lid and let them get to know each other for about five minutes.

Serve in a beautiful ceramic bowl with almost anything—vegetables, yogurt, chutney, and salad. Have enough nuts to enhance the rice—not too much or too little. Use your intuition.

Stir-fry spinach

If you like (and even if you do not like) spinach—here is a quick one. You need:

Spinach
Olive oil
Garlic
Salt and pepper to taste

Wash the spinach well and tear it with your fingers. Set aside. Peel and cut the garlic into small pieces. Heat the olive oil in a pan, and add garlic. When the garlic is browned well, add the spinach, keeping the flame medium to high, and stirring all the time. Bring the spinach at the bottom of the pan to the top of the pan, moving it all the time with a spatula. Add salt and black pepper to taste. And, if you like it hot, add red pepper.

Remove from the flame and serve with steamed rice. Add some soy sauce to the rice. Eat in a ceramic bowl, with chopsticks, if you can manage them.

An afternoon debriefing

Two days ago, I was part of a debriefing session on the riots that rocked Kabul in May, when an American convoy, coming south on the Jalalabad road during the morning rush hour, ran into several cars due to brake failure.

Facilitated by Heather McCoy, a professional counsellor/ therapist practicing in Kabul, eight of us (seven expats and one Afghan) gathered in the sitting room of our shared house. Three others who were supposed to be with us, were missing—two were out of town and one was in a meeting.

With a temperature of 42° outside, the dark, somewhat cooler room provided a comfortable sanctuary for what we were about to begin. During those fateful days, riots broke out, people were injured, houses and cars were burned, and shops were looted. There was a 9:00 p.m. to 6:00 a.m. curfew for a whole week. It was the worst case of violence in Kabul since 2001 when the Taliban were ousted.

I was looking forward to the session, which had been planned for a month. Besides being trained as a clinical hypnotherapist, I like psychological processes. The session was scheduled for 90 minutes, clearly not long enough. Heather introduced us to, and guided us through, processes that we generally experience after a traumatic event—feelings, thoughts, physical symptoms and behaviour. I recognised some of these in my own reactions during and after the events of May 29. I could feel the memories of that day and the following days coming back—memories which I had chosen to forget, or push to the back of my mind. Each of us gave our versions of what happened to those around us as we remembered it, some expressing themselves more than others.

I recalled the confusion, helplessness and sadness I had felt at the futility of it all. I remember thinking: who is this going to benefit? Everyone loses. Not just the Afghans, but also the international community of which I was a part.

My outlet, was my blog among other things. I wrote almost every day. I also had the advantage of having studied and practised energy healing. These helped me keep myself and others around me together. I took on the role of the 'elder', consoling and counselling them in my own way. It gave me something to do. It also took my mind off how I was feeling.

The debriefing was accompanied by cherry and orange juice, pies and chocolate cake from the French bakery, alongside green tea and melon. Heather didn't eat or drink very much. I felt much better after the debriefing, and also somewhat lighter. I wrote a blog, sent emails, showered and went out for dinner with my housemates. We didn't speak about the debriefing.

Other such sessions were conducted with the Afghan staff, that I heard also went well. At some point, the information of the experiences of the two groups—Afghans and expats—would be shared with each other.

There were many theories about the incidents post-May 29. Some analysts say the disturbances were not premeditated, unlike the last major riots that had occurred in Kabul a year earlier. In May 2005, anti-US demonstrations engulfed Kabul and many other cities in Afghanistan, mainly in protest against a story in the US-based magazine, *Newsweek* about some interrogators at the US detention facility in Guantanamo Bay, Cuba, allegedly desecrating the Koran. That year's riots were very well-coordinated and seemed to have an agenda.

Several observers concluded that the 2006 riots were spontaneous and were sparked by the accident. At the same time, there was enough built-up frustration to fuel the riotous protests beyond the initial destructive day; pent up frustration from decades of trauma, loss, sadness and feeling of futility.

The nature of friendship

Friendships in Afghanistan, especially among the expats, develop quickly. There is a shared purpose in being in the country, and time after work can be spent with friends without the responsibilities of home and family. One friend I made here was Grace.

I met Grace at a World Press Freedom Day function, co-hosted by my training centre. She was standing by a table when I went up and introduced myself to her.

It was difficult to miss her. She is tall, slim, and has very short dark hair. As we began to talk, I found out that it was her third day in Kabul. We met several times after that, both professionally and socially. I took her to my favourite places in Kabul—La Fontaine, the Herat Carpet Centre, the Kabul Serena and the Intercontinental. Four days after the riots, we were at the Intercontinental and decided to get a foot massage. There was no room for us, the Thai receptionist said. But I persisted, and in ten minutes, we were both in. Two days later, there was a bomb blast at the hotel; on the very floor where we had our foot massages.

Last night, I went to her house for the first time as I was in India when she moved in. It was a lovely place with a garden. We walked through the house and I could not resist planning her interiors: a carpet here, I said, a wall hanging here; a plant by this window and an artefact here, and there. I was taking over! She took it well, and laughed at my enthusiasm. We sat in the verandah, next to the giant satellite dish that had been installed the same day. We didn't let it stop us from enjoying the cool air, the sunflowers, and when the light faded, the moon and the stars. We had gin and tonics with slices of lime, cheese, crackers and olives. Grace told me about her Dubai trip, and I told her about my work and imminent departure to India.

Over dinner, we shared our stories—how we became the people we are today—the learning, the pain, the growth, and what we dreamed about. What brought us to Afghanistan, and what keeps us here. We talked about mutual friends and acquaintances and their experiences of coping with living in Afghanistan, or life in general. We talked about how lucky we were that we could travel openly and not be locked down and 'compounded' like some of our expat friends.

The lights were dim and were getting dimmer because of the low voltage. Grace didn't like the sound of the generator, so we enjoyed the dim light. After dinner, we moved back to the verandah to enjoy the moonlight. We made plans for Friday—kilim and carpet shops, lunch and then—who knows! It was an evening of shared experiences, laughter, and gentle peace.

Cooking and having friends over

In the old days, growing up in India, we had parties—tea parties, dinner parties, and cocktails. I grew up in West Bengal and my father worked for a British company. Parties were a

British legacy that I quite liked, except that it is not a part of my vocabulary anymore, having been replaced by get-togethers.

On Thursday, I invited four people, Gunther, Hans, Rupert, and Vijay, for dinner. The first three are German and Vijay is an Indian by birth but grew up in America. We all met for the first time in Kabul. I'm a bit of a planner and think of people who would enjoy each other's company.

While Rupert could not make it because of a serious case of parasites and was leaving for Germany, Italy, and France that night, Vijay and Gunther arrived within minutes of each other. Turned out that they actually lived in the same guest house and occasionally chatted with each other! "I didn't know *you* were coming", they said, laughing. Hans, the final guest for the night, arrived shortly.

I came home at 4:00 p.m. and rested for half an hour. Then went down to the kitchen and got ready to cook. The menu was rice with nuts and raisins, tomato chutney, sautéed spinach and beans, and yogurt raita. I washed and cut the spinach and beans, the ginger and garlic, and spring onions. Boiled the tomatoes, removed their skins, and mashed them—for the tomato chutney. In hot oil, the mustard seeds popped with the whole cumin. I added tomatoes, salt, pepper, dried dates, and a pinch of sugar. And when it was done, I added a handful of freshly cut spring onions.

I sautéed the spinach in oil, some pods of browned garlic, and a green chilli. I boiled the beans and sautéed them in ginger, salt and pepper. I grated the cucumber, adding yogurt, garam masala, a little red pepper and mint, and set it in the refrigerator. Then, I washed the rice several times in cool water, getting it ready to be cooked when we started to eat. A handful of almonds, walnuts, and raisins were washed and kept aside.

I had planned to sit out in the garden, a white tablecloth over the table, under the stars and moon. Hans, in a short-sleeved sports shirt, was sniffing and said he was afraid of the mosquitoes. Gunther joked about Hans's caution. We decided to stay indoors and sat around the dining table where I had laid out hummus, black and green olives, crackers and cheese—in my Istalif pottery. Vijay opted for red wine; Rupert white; and Gunther had a beer. I got a vodka and fresh lime for myself. As the evening wore on, we caught glimpses of the setting sun through the dining room window. The breeze was strong and it got cooler as time passed. The conversation focused on Afghanistan, as it always did.

Our dining room leads into the kitchen. As I sat listening to talk about warlords, politics, and language, I realised I had forgotten to cut the mangoes. So, I took three mangoes from the refrigerator into the kitchen, washed, peeled, and cut them. I could hear the guys in the other room, talking in low voices, in intense discussion, and in between—laughter. As the very sweet aroma of the mangoes wafted to my nostrils, I gave thanks—for friends, for food, for Afghanistan and the home I lived in.

Around 8.30 p.m., I started the rice, sautéed the nuts and raisins and began to heat the spinach and beans. My guests helped bring in the plates, forks, and dinner. I remembered to offer them the mango pickles, which were promptly accepted by Gunther and Vijay.

The talk turned to lighter things—shared houses in Kabul, housemates, guards, cats, personalities, etc. There was a lot of laughter, all good fun. I served the mangoes, and the talk shifted to types and origins of different mango varieties.

It was time for herbal tea and Italian coffee and, eventually, time to leave. I walked my quests to the car; hugs and kisses were exchanged, and promises to meet in the near future—whenever and wherever that was.

Upset and apologies

I am upset because someone is upset with me. It is Najiba, the ex-assistant who recently got married. An Afghan colleague, who did not go to the wedding, requested me to send her a few pictures of the wedding. As I was doing this, I thought why not send it to the office e-list? However, after having sent the pictures, I found out that apparently, this was not appropriate behaviour. Afghan women are not meant to be photographed. I heard people mention this in the corridors of the training centre over the next few days and recalled how Najiba would turn her face away from the camera when we took group photographs at the end of our training courses. But not all women did this.

This morning, Najiba sent an email to the centre e-list, asking us to delete her wedding photographs from our computers. I was surprised and confused. Someone explained to me that there are many Afghan conventions and customs that I do not follow. I do not cover my head, in public or private. I greet my expat male friends in public with a hug and/or a cheek-to-cheek peck. I touch people, also something that I am not supposed to do.

I have always questioned tradition and norms. Do they make sense to me, I ask myself? In my training sessions, often the response is: Islam does not allow this or we do not do it like this, etc. My response has been that all religions, traditions were created a long time ago, and probably made sense at that time. Our responsibility, as individuals and groups, is to ask if that tradition works for us in the present. In a country where so much has changed, much remains the same. Men are very much in control, and women suffer, mostly silently. It is complex and complicated.

I know what works for me. But I didn't feel good about Najiba being upset because of something I had done, wittingly or unwittingly. So I emailed Najiba an apology this afternoon.

Last day in Kabul

My last day in Kabul was quite perfect.

I had tea in the garden, coffee with Aleksandr (who returned from Belarus two nights ago), and we went to the training centre. I chatted with my colleagues and we had lunch together. There was a small farewell for me where Salim made a speech that had me in tears. The staff presented me with an amethyst pendant and a bracelet, and a wonderful platter of fruits—grapes and peaches—sat in the middle of the lunch table.

It was 1:30 p.m., and Aziz was waiting to take me to Chicken Street. The Nuristani cupboard was polished and ready, as were the spice boxes—red and orange, with intricate carving.

Next was the kilim shop—two Uzbeki kilim runners for my sisters and a smaller square one for myself. Oh, I must have this Iranian kilim—square, 2x2′—and so fine. Money handed over, salaams exchanged, goodbyes said, I felt sad that I would not be seeing Wahid for some time.

Aziz had already put the cupboard in the car. I threw in the kilims. Have you had lunch, I asked Aziz? Sort of, he said. I mean, yes or no Aziz, what is sort of? He laughed. I suggested we go to Dan's Le Bistro, which we had not seen yet. This is Dan's, of La Fontaine fame, new eatery. We find it soon, and it is lovely—an old home with kilims and carpets on the floor, walls, and tables. It has large windows and plain crockery, and a great bar with four plain, chic drop-lights.

Where's Dan, I ask the waiter? Sleeping, he says. Aziz and I take a table and order. Dan arrives in 30 minutes. He joins us and offers his special treat—cherry dessert with custard. We can't, and do not, say no. An Afghan parliamentary friend of Dan's arrives, and we settle down with whisky. The talk, as always, turns to Afghanistan.

I went home, had a quick shower and Miriam and Adele arrived. It was our last meal together and they had organised a surprise for me. We went to the Indian restaurant. Who is coming, I asked them, but they wouldn't tell me. As we were seated in the restaurant, Grace, Caroline, Gunther and a German journalist from Bangkok joined us. Jan joined up as we started with the snacks. We order chicken tikka, tandoori chicken, aloo chaat, kadhai paneer, mutton biryani and assorted breads.

I wanted my friends to see Dan's place. He closed at 10, but said he would wait for us. Caroline and Grace begged off, and the rest of us went. At night, the restaurant had taken on a warm glowing air. Dan had lamps on the tables. We settled by a large window and pulled chairs around. There was chocolate cake (with custard), cognac, and coffee. It was wonderful. I was gifted two beautiful glass lamps by Adele and Miriam.

As we headed home, the sky was full of stars and a bright moon. There was no electricity at home, but I was ready for bed. A perfect end to a perfect day.

A country in conflict

As I was leaving Afghanistan in July 2006, the security situation was deteriorating. In August NATO troops took over the leadership of military operations in the south. There was fierce fighting as the forces tried to extend government control in areas where Taliban influence was strong. By October, NATO had responsibility for security across the whole of Afghanistan, and took additional command of the US-led coalition in the east of the country.

The Taliban emerged in the early 1990s in northern Pakistan following the withdrawal of the Soviet troops from Afghanistan. A predominantly Pashtun movement, the Taliban assisted covertly by the U.S., came to prominence in Afghanistan in the autumn of 1994. It is commonly believed that they first appeared in religious seminaries—mostly paid for by money from Saudi Arabia—which preached a hardline form of Sunni Islam.

Pakistan has repeatedly denied that it is the architect of the Taliban enterprise, but there is little doubt that many Afghans who initially joined the movement were educated in madrassas in Pakistan. It was also one of the only three countries, along with Saudi Arabia and the United Arab Emirates (UAE), that recognised the Taliban when they were in power in Afghanistan from the mid-1990s until 2001; and the last country to break diplomatic ties with them.

In recent years, the Taliban have re-emerged in Afghanistan and grown far stronger in Pakistan, where observers say there is a loose co-ordination between different Taliban factions and militant groups. The main Pakistani faction was led by Hakimullah Mehsud until his death. His party, Tehrik-i-Taliban Pakistan (TTP) is blamed for dozens of suicide bombings and other attacks. Observers however, warn against over-stating the existence of one unified insurgency against the Pakistani state.

The Taliban in Afghanistan are still believed to be led by Mullah Omar, a village clergyman who lost his right eye fighting the occupying forces of the Soviet Union in the 1980s.

How were Afghans faring during this time? It depends on

whom you ask. Since 2004, a democracy assessment survey has been carried out to establish an accurate and long-term barometer of public opinion across Afghanistan to help assess the direction in which the country is moving in the post-Taliban era.

The 2006 survey of the Afghan people conducted by the Asia Foundation found that some 44 per cent of respondents said things were moving in the right direction, 21 per cent said they were moving in the wrong direction and another 29 per cent had mixed feelings. Good security was cited as the biggest reason for the country going in the right direction (31 per cent), followed by peace (29 per cent), and disarmament (26 per cent).[15]

The major national-level problems were a poor economy, uncertain security situation, slow pace of reconstruction -development, and unemployment. Eighty per cent felt the government was doing a good job, but most of the credit in this regard went to the education and health sectors, while the government was seen to be performing below par in employment generation, economic revival and fighting corruption.

Perceptions towards institutions varied widely. More than 80 per cent of the people had a fair amount of confidence in institutions such as the Afghan National Police (ANP) and Afghan National Army (ANA). This was followed by electronic media, shuras and jirgas, provincial councils, international NGOs, and community development councils (CDCs). But less than half the respondents had confidence in the government's justice system, political parties, and local militias. Perception of the prevalence of corruption was higher at the national level (74 per cent) than at the provincial (60 per cent) or local levels (48 per cent).

Eighty per cent of the people thought poppy cultivation was wrong. Of these, 50 per cent cited religion as the reason, while 35 per cent cited opium addiction. Linkages to terrorism and insecurity were cited by 10 per cent or less of the people.

Fifty-four per cent of the respondents felt that they were more prosperous now than under the Taliban regime, while 26 per cent felt less so, and 12 per cent felt that there had been no change.

Democracy for most people in Afghanistan (51 per cent) means freedom, followed by peace (33 per cent). For a significant proportion of them, it also means rights and laws (26 per cent), followed by government of the people (25 per cent). Most hold the opinion that democracy is not antithetical to Islam. Sixty-six per cent believe that democracy can be Islamic, while 29 per cent believe that it challenges Islamic values.

Sixty per cent of Afghans are of the opinion that religious leaders should be consulted; only 36 per cent think that politics and religion should not mix. Seventy-three per cent of them are satisfied with the way democracy works in the country.

Twenty-nine per cent identified lack of education as the biggest problem facing women in Afghanistan today. Another 13 per cent identified lack of women's rights as the biggest problem, followed by the lack of job opportunities for women (9 per cent). Opposition to women in leadership positions in various political bodies is in the range of 39 to 44 per cent; the opposition is highest in national parliament (44 per cent) and lowest in district development assemblies (39 per cent).

2008

Someone brings material for an explosion
Someone is a suicide bomber
Someone has cut off my finger for voting
God, would you listen to my pain?

– Rahela Yar, Afghan poet

Brokering peace

Efforts to bring peace to Afghanistan continue.

In September, on the day of Eid, President Karzai said he had repeatedly sought the intervention of Saudi Arabia to bring the Taliban to the negotiating table. On the same day, Mullah Omar called on Afghans to continue the holy war against foreign troops. According to *The Economist*, King Abdullah hosted a Ramadan breakfast with representatives from the Afghan government and the Taliban, at the end of September, but both sides denied that any real negotiations took place.

A month later, Pashtun tribal leaders from Afghanistan and Pakistan were scheduled to meet in Islamabad for a "jirgagai" (mini-jirga) to discuss tackling militant violence. No representatives from the Taliban were present. A draft recommendation in a White House assessment of Afghan strategy called for talks between the Afghan government and the Taliban, with US participation, an idea supported by Gen. David Petraeus, who publicly endorsed talks with "less extreme Taliban elements". The Afghan government, too, was actively pursuing the possibility of peace talks with the Taliban and other insurgent groups.

According to *The Washington Post*, President Karzai offered Mullah Omar safe passage for negotiations in November, saying he would resist demands to hand the Taliban leader over to US authorities. Taliban spokesman Zabiullah Mujahid responded that the Taliban "will not take part in any peace talks with Karzai ... until such a day when foreign forces leave Afghanistan".

The Afghan study tour

In January 2008, I joined Facebook and, in an experimental mood, started a page on health and wellness. An Afghan woman, Noor, became friends with me on Facebook and we exchanged messages. In August, she asked if I could suggest someone to organise a study tour on violence against women. I said that I could try.

Afghans were already working hard on the issue of violence against women. A preliminary survey had been conducted with the intention of introducing suitable legislation in parliament. Participants in the study tour wanted to personally witness and hear from individuals and organisations in India about their experiences. I offered to work with Noor on the study tour, and after several rounds of communication and details, we had a plan. I asked a UN agency in Delhi for information on who was doing what, as they had coordinated a great deal of work on domestic violence in the South Asian region. They were immensely helpful and suggested that I also meet their Afghanistan Country Director who was coming to town in a few days.

International media regularly carried news about violence against women in Afghanistan. In September 2008, a month before the study tour, Malalai Kakar, the highest-ranking female police officer in Kandahar, was killed, allegedly because she was leading a unit of ten policewomen against domestic violence.

Over the next week, I drew up a list of people and organisations the Afghan participants in the study tour could meet, contacted them, and followed up with phone calls. Noor and I developed a background document on the goals of the study tour and the profiles of the five women who would be attending. I handled all the logistics to ensure that they had a comfortable week-long stay in Delhi and stationed them at a Bed and Breakfast in Vasant Kunj that is run by my friend, Rita.

The week was very full. We drove around Delhi to the appointments; Indians described their work and the Afghans listened and asked questions. Noor introduced the group and their mission and translated back and forth in English and Dari. I designed and conducted a day's training on domestic violence advocacy work, also incorporating some healing techniques.

I had learnt on my visits to Afghanistan that no Afghan was untouched or immune from trauma as a result of decades of war and conflict. As we drove around for our appointments, the participants spoke softly and rapidly in Dari, but I could sense strong emotions, some tears and them comforting each other. During the week they bonded among themselves, and with me. They did not know each other very well before they came to Delhi, but by the time they left they had discovered new sides to each other. They told their stories, cried, laughed, soothed each other, and got really close. By the time we went into the all-day advocacy workshop, I felt that I knew them fairly well.

Before they left, Noor asked if I could assist them in designing a three-year strategy for their work on violence against women, an offer I was happy to accept. The week had taken me back to Afghanistan without my actually being there.

Violence against women in Afghanistan

A 2009 United Nations Assistance Mission in Afghanistan (UNAMA) and United Nations High Commissioner for Refugees (UNHCR) report on violence against women stated that violence, in public and private, is an everyday occurrence in the lives of many Afghan women.

Rape and sexual violence, including in detention facilities, so-called "honour" killings, the exchange of women and girls as a form of dispute resolution (often in connection with land or property issues), trafficking and abduction, early and forced marriages, domestic violence, as well as threats or attacks against women in public life, are but some of the problems that many Afghan women have to endure.

Acute violence poses an immediate threat to the safety and physical integrity of women and girls. There are cultural, social, and other norms that reproduce gender biases and dictate the subservient role accorded to women. Although some practices such as *baad* (a custom in Pakistan and Afghanistan among Pashtun tribes, in which a young virgin from the culprit's family is traded to help settle a dispute on behalf of her older relatives) precede Islam, religion is often used to reinforce these traditions that are not sanctioned by Islamic precepts.

Harmful traditional practices, also preceding Islam, have been reinforced by tribal, community, and religious leaders in the name of religion. However, as acknowledged in the UNAMA and UNHCR report, the concept of 'tradition' has to be treated with a degree of caution, as

> What to western eyes looks like tradition, is in many instances the manifestation of new and more brutal forms of subjugation of the weak, made possible by a commodified criminal economy, total lack of security, and the erosion of bonds of trust and solidarity that were tested to the limit by war, social upheaval, and poverty.

As a result, many communities and families sincerely believe that women should stay at home. A popular Afghan saying encapsulates this: "Women are made for homes or graves."

The tradition of segregating the sexes reinforces this belief.

In many cases, women in public life have indicated that they suffer from immense strain, with many opting for a low profile, even if this means resigning from their positions rather than facing constant pressure mainly from male relatives, colleagues, and community members.

After the study tour on violence against women in 2008, a number of prominent Afghan women's rights activists, members of civil society groups, and lawmakers drafted a bill to protect women through legal channels and to define crimes of violence against women. The bill, known as The Elimination of Violence against Women (EVAW) Law, was decreed into law through an executive order by the President Hamid Karzai on July 20, 2009, while parliament was in recess. During such periods, the Afghan constitution allows the president to issue decrees for emergency purposes, but it also requires such decrees to be forwarded to parliament for approval.

The law was tabled in parliament but did not pass, and, as of 2015, the fate of the EVAW law continues to remain undecided.

2009: Developments in diplomacy

Talks between Afghanistan, other member nations, and the Taliban continued.

According to *The New York Times*, in March 2009, the Afghan government was reportedly in preliminary discussions with Taliban representatives to discuss the potential for negotiations. In August, the Afghan presidential candidates weighed in on talks with the Taliban. Karzai vocally supported negotiations, and promised to hold a tribal gathering with the Taliban and Gulbuddin Hekmatyar, if re-elected. Abdullah Abdullah and Ashraf Ghani said grassroots approaches through community and tribal councils must come first, and Mr. Ghani advocated ceasefire as the next step before peace negotiations.

August: the Five Million Women Campaign

In July this year, Noor, the person I organised the study tour for, posted a notice about the Five Million Women Campaign (5MWC) on Facebook.

My friend Rita had her own history with Afghanistan. She had visited her father, a musician, when he had lived and travelled in Afghanistan in the 1970s. Rita often talked about making a documentary in Afghanistan, and the 5MWC seemed like a good subject. Let's go to Afghanistan and cover the 5MWC, I suggested to Rita. We called Noor, rapidly wrote a concept note with a budget and shared it with her. We knew we were going to have to finance this leg of the work ourselves. Tickets bought, visas acquired, we set off on August 1.

We had two weeks to prepare for the trip. Numerous e-mails and phone calls were made to organise camera people, equipment, car and driver; interpreters were sent to people and organisations I had known from my earlier trips. They generously gave of their time and energy, suggesting other people we could follow-up with. We left for Kabul, some things under our belt but also many loose ends.

Marie, an American woman who was working in Kabul, offered us a place to stay in her home. She suggested we use her caretaker, Wasim, to assist us. Wasim was a wonder. He doubled, tripled and quadrupled up as our driver, translator, facilitator, counsellor, jester and, sometimes, even director! He was fluent in Dari, Urdu, Hindi, English, and even Punjabi. His greatest asset: he never said no.

It was good to be back in Afghanistan. My last trip here had been in 2006. The airport had been renovated. As we stood in line in a brand new building, immigration was a breeze. While changing money, the man behind the counter said that the airport building was re-done by the Japanese for 45 million dollars, and that it could have been better. It looks like a warehouse, he stated. All airports look like this, I said.

Driving through the streets to Taimani, the neighbourhood where Marie lived, some of the main roads had been tarred and traffic flowed well. The amazing thing in Kabul is that no matter how bad the traffic is, Afghans do not honk, unlike us Indians. It is a quiet navigation through traffic. There were many more cars on the streets than there were three years ago.

Our ten days were full of scheduled meetings, discussions, and some shooting. The camera we took from India had problems (a tape got stuck) and we had to rent one from a local agency, facilitated by my friend and colleague, Omar.

What was the Five Million Women Campaign? It was a campaign, riding on the presidential and provincial elections slated for August 20, to get women involved in politics, called out to them to register to vote and stand for office.

The registered voting population of Afghanistan was estimated to be between 15 million and 17 million. Of these, 38 per cent, or over six million, were women. The AWN, International Foundation for Electoral Systems (IFES), and other groups collaborating in the 5MWC hoped that at least five million of these six million women would eventually participate in the Afghan elections. Thus the name: The Five Million Women Campaign.

We attended several meetings of the 5MWC, including the August 4 gathering, when 1,500 women from Kabul and the provinces gathered in the Loya Jirga Tent. Each woman

Election poster

was given a green scarf, and looking out into the crowd from the podium, there was a sea of green. Everyone in the tent, including men, wore green scarves.

On the same day, the Taliban launched seven rockets in Kabul's residential areas, further terrorising people scarred by rampant insecurity. The women's gathering was a brave demonstration of their belief that they have the right to participate in their country's politics and have a say in the way they are governed.

During our stay in Kabul, most people we interacted with were focused on the elections. We met with women's organisations, the AWN, journalists, the UN staff, and other people involved in the elections. Opinions on the elections varied—from cynicism to optimism. Media were full of news about the elections, from the capital to the provinces. There were roundtable discussions on TV between candidates and civil society members. Rumours, gossip, and factual information were all in circulation.

Around Kabul, there was a festive mood: election posters, faces of the candidates standing for elections, vans moving around the city with young men spilling out of them, waving flags and pamphlets, rooting for their candidates and parties.

Moving around in Kabul, Rita began recognising the places she had frequented. We drove down the street where she had lived with her family, and the house was still there. We stopped to take pictures, and she even thought she would come back and request the current residents to let her see the apartment. It didn't happen. She recalled her Dari and bought a phrase book to polish her skills.

It was good to be back. I met up with friends and visited the training centre I was based at in 2006. It was quiet, as they had just ended a training with media on how to cover elections. I went back to the naan shop on the street I lived on and was greeted with such familiarity that it seemed like I was there the day before.

I felt that since 2006, when I was last in Kabul, there was distinct signs of activity and optimism. According to the Asian Foundation Survey of the Afghan people, the year 2009 brought a certain renewed confidence in the electoral process. Seventy per cent of respondents said they believed that voting could lead to improvement, reversing the trend of the last two years. There was a steady rise in the proportion of respondents who said they had some degree of influence over government decisions—from 36 per cent in 2006 to 42 per cent in 2009.[16]

There was a significant rise in public confidence in a number of election-related institutions, including the Independent Election Commission (from 58 per cent in 2008 to 67 per cent in 2009) and political parties (47 per cent, which is the highest recorded figure since 2006).

The survey was conducted in June 2009 with the presidential and provincial council elections scheduled for August. Two months before the elections, 82 per cent of respondents were aware of the elections and 77 per cent had registered to vote. Voter registration was significantly higher among men (85 per cent) than women (69 per cent). Around three-quarters (73 per cent) of those who had not registered said they did not know where to do so.

The proportion of respondents who reported having no interest in participating in the elections rose sharply in 2009, and has more than doubled since 2004 (from 12 per cent to 16 per cent in 2005, 18 per cent in 2008 and 26 per cent in 2009). Security concerns were also prevalent (18 per cent), particularly in the south-east (25 per cent) and south-west (30 per cent).

Sixty-four per cent of respondents said that the upcoming elections would be free and fair. Those who thought otherwise identified a range of potential problems, including cheating in the vote count (39 per cent) and buying of votes (33 per cent). Only a small proportion mentioned intimidation against voters or party activists (8 per cent). Doubts about the elections being free and fair were highest in the south-west (37 per cent), south-east (29 per cent), central/Kabul (25 per cent) and western (23 per cent) regions.

While Afghanistan has a constitution and due process of law, much of the country has a deep belief in traditional systems of conflict resolution. Religious leaders continue to play a major role in local communities. According to the survey, support for consultation with religious leaders in government decision-making and to resolve local problems continues to rise, with the highest levels of support in the east (82 per cent), and the south-west (72 per cent) of the country.

Stated support for gender equality remains high, including equal educational opportunities (87 per cent) and women's right to vote (83 per cent). The proportion who say that women should be allowed to work outside the home has decreased marginally each year from 71 per cent in 2006 to its lowest level in 2009 (67 per cent).

The Afghan constitution guarantees that "from each province on average at least two female delegates shall have membership in the Wolesi Jirga," therefore guaranteeing women 68 seats (27 per cent) in the 249 member Wolesi Jirga. Similarly, the Afghan election law contains a provision that at least 25 per cent of seats in provincial councils must be reserved for women.

Results in 2009 showed a significant decline in support for female representation in governance bodies at all levels, compared to previous years. During our visit, we heard numerous stories of how women candidates were humiliated and threatened by men and political parties. Despite the fact that there is a constitutional provision for women in politics, there is a deep-rooted feeling that women belong in the home.

Conservative interpretations and misinterpretations of Islam similarly shape Afghans' perceptions regarding what is permissible for a woman. Religious and community leaders retain immense power in influencing, if not dictating, peoples' attitudes.

Working outside the home is said by some mullahs to be disrespectful of Islam. A female MP says, "I was warned not to work, because a female working outside the home is taboo;

and that it is forbidden by Sharia. The salary I receive is haram (illegitimate) and I must stay at home." A provincial council member added that some mullahs label husbands of such women as kafir, or infidels.

Grapes in Charikar, Parwan

On one Sunday, Wasim (who was assisting Rita and me in the documentary production) and I drove north to Parwan province, which straddles Kabul province. Leaving behind Kabul traffic and urban activity, the drive was spectacular, with mountains and mud architecture dotting the sides of the highway and an open road.

Soon, the grape vines appeared. See the grapes, Wasim pointed out. How come they are hanging so low, I asked? He told me that the grapes found here were of special quality, better than the one on the vines. Once in Charikar, the capital of Parwan province, we went to the kebab shop that Shahir, a Kabul-based friend, had mentioned the night before.

Satiated with all the good food, we walked into the street and around the markets. I love markets, especially in smaller towns—the shops are open and you get to see their wares. There was an old man selling spices, beans, legumes out in the open, for everyone to see. There were stands with tomatoes, radishes, apricots, onions, and melons. A pavement vendor selling soap, a man who fixes shoes with an array of nails, glues, and shoe polishes, and a donkey piled with local greens.

Finally, we came upon the grapes—a heavenly purple-burgundy in colour, luscious and large. Let's get some, I said to Wasim. We bought a kilo of grapes and a kilo of the local soft flushed apricots, zardaloos.

Wasim suggested we go back to Kabul via Istalif, the hill

Zardaloos/apricots in Parwan market

town. "My uncle is the local MP", said Wasim, "and my aunt would love to meet you." I had visited Istalif several times during my stay in Afghanistan in 2006 and loved the place. Oh yes, I said, immediately thinking about the pottery I could buy.

We passed his uncle and aunt's house as we drove up the winding road to Istalif. "That's my uncle, the bald guy," said Wasim, pointing to a poster stuck on the wall. Wasim has a thing about baldness. Only 28, he is already balding and is very worried about this! We stopped at the mazar, with beautiful old trees and watched a group of women who were eating and chatting excitedly behind a makeshift curtain.

After the mazar, we ran into Dr. Abdullah Abdullah's presidential campaign meeting. Wasim's uncle being the local

MP meant that we got security to move us all the way up to the main podium. I was one of only three women (the other two being foreign correspondents) in a sea of men.

After the excitement, we stopped at Wasim's aunt's house and sat under the trees by a small stream, surrounded by greenery and flowers. Wasim's aunt brought out some lunch and—would you believe it—a lovely bowl of grapes! The bowl was handcrafted in Istalif and the grapes were from their vineyard. Wasim was not hungry, but his cousin and I tucked into the meal and chatted.

The grapes were purple and not genetically modified, which meant that they came in various shapes and sizes. I loved this. As you took a bite, a small seed popped out. This could be swallowed as well, if you were feeling lazy. When we got home to Marie's place, I washed the grapes I had bought in Parwan, put them in an Istalif bowl and placed them next to her as she worked at her computer.

I loved the kebabs, the walk in the markets, seeing and buying the fruit, and then bringing it home to share with friends. Wish you could have some!

2010–2011: Post-elections and reconciliation efforts

Shortly after I left Kabul, Afghans went to vote in the presidential elections on August 20. Incumbent Hamid Karzai won with a 49.67 per cent of the vote, and Abdullah Abdullah finished second with 30.5 per cent.

According to reports, the election was characterised by a lack of security, low voter turnout, poor awareness about the election and widespread ballot stuffing, intimidation, and other electoral frauds.

Afghanistan shares many characteristics with other so-called post-conflict countries. These include a young political system, a weak institutional set-up, a relatively large role for the 'international community', and a vulnerable and contested security situation. These challenges directly affect the nature of the elections. The novelty and opportunity that elections provide for political positioning has led to a proliferation of candidates, making it more difficult for voters to make up their minds. The relative weakness of institutions has allowed for a continued dominance of patronage politics. An unevenly implemented disarmament programme, coupled with trends towards rearmament (through private security companies and 'community-based' security initiatives), and the weakness of the rule of law institutions, means that there is a continued threat of violence and intimidation. An active and effective insurgency, well entrenched in the south and the south-east and branching out into the west and the north, limits the government's access in considerable parts of the country and threatens to disenfranchise parts of the electorate.[17]

The challenges to institutionalising elections as a democratic procedure in Afghanistan are numerous. The most prominent are the security situation, a lack of mechanisms to encourage meaningful party participation, weak state institutions, and a lack of universal impartiality within government authorities. In addition, three major socio-economic challenges influence the success (or lack thereof) of election participation and institutionalisation in Afghanistan: illiteracy, poverty, and women's unequal status in Afghan society.[18]

The UN, American and Afghan officials hailed the election as a success, while evidence from observers on the ground and media suggested that the Taliban had succeeded in deterring many Afghans from voting.

A second round run-off vote, announced under heavy US

and ally pressure, was originally scheduled for November 7, 2009, but was cancelled after Abdullah Abdullah refused to participate. Hamid Karzai was declared the President of Afghanistan for another five year term.

The election was the second under the present constitution of Afghanistan and was held on the same day as elections for 34 council seats. The Taliban called for a boycott of the election, calling it a "programme of the crusaders" and "an American process".

In the post-2009 election period, there was much talk and activity regarding engaging with the Taliban. According to *The New York Times*, in January 2010, Afghan and Taliban officials had secret talks in the Maldives. The Taliban's leadership council released a statement rejecting peace talks and calling for the withdrawal of foreign forces. Mohammad Masoom Stanekzai, in charge of reconciliation talks, dismissed Taliban denials and said contact between the government and the Taliban has occurred and will continue.

According to the *Wall Street Journal*, President Karzai travelled to Saudi Arabia to try and revive peace talks with the Taliban leadership. Mullah Abdul Ghani Baradar, allegedly head of the Taliban's political arm and chief military strategist, was captured in Pakistan. At home, there was some displeasure at President Karzai's pursuing high-level talks and reconciliation with the Taliban and alienated leaders of Afghanistan's largest ethnic minority groups.[19]

In October 2010, US forces reportedly facilitated the passage of senior Taliban leaders to Kabul in support of talks between the Afghan government and the Taliban leadership. And, in November, according to *The New York Times*, a man claiming to be the Taliban official, Mullah Akhtar Muhammad

Mansour, was revealed as an impostor, dashing hopes of progress in the peace talks.

Meanwhile, the insurgency continued. The UN reported that 2010 was the deadliest year so far for Afghan civilians in nearly a decade of warfare. The UN mission in Afghanistan put the number of civilians killed at 2,777, a 15 per cent increase from the previous year. About three-quarters of those deaths were caused by insurgents, the report said. Most of the civilian casualties were capriciously random in nature, with hundreds of people dying in suicide attacks or roadside bombings.

But the report also noted an ominous trend: a doubling in the number of assassinations of government officials, tribal elders and other prominent figures. These targeted killings are viewed as an unambiguous warning by insurgents against cooperating with the administration of President Hamid Karzai or with western military forces.

The civilian deaths and injuries were concentrated in the principal conflict zones—the south and east—but touched all areas of the country. There was an increase in violence in some areas that had been previously considered relatively peaceful, such as the north.

In February 2011, *The New York Times* reported that President Karzai had called for the release of Taliban official Mullah Khairullah Khairkhwa from Guantanamo Bay, to join in the reconciliation talks. In April, Mohammad Masoom Stanekzai confirmed that the government had been engaged in reconciliation talks with the Taliban for some time, with the support of the US. In May, US officials reportedly participated in meetings with a high-level Taliban official, Tayeb Agha (who had been arrested by Pakistani authorities the previous year and released). In June, President Karzai publicly asserted

US involvement in talks with the Taliban, and the US Defense Secretary, Robert Gates, confirmed that the US was involved in the early stages of such talks. According to the *Washington Post*, Secretary of State Hillary Clinton called the talks "very preliminary".

In a startling turn of events, according to ABC news reports, in a covert operation on May 2, 2011, US Navy SEALs (a special operations force) and CIA operatives killed Osama bin Laden in his residential compound in Abbottabad, Pakistan. Al-Qaeda swore to avenge bin Laden's death. A statement posted on jihadist websites stated, "We will remain, God willing, a curse chasing the Americans and their agents, following them outside and inside their countries."

Back in the US, as pressure had been mounting to pull troops out of Afghanistan, President Obama announced in June 2011, that the US would begin withdrawing military forces from Afghanistan and transferring responsibility for security to the Afghan National Security Forces (ANSF). The US goal was to be substantially out of Afghanistan by 2014, with ANSF responsible for the entire country. Obama further said that 10,000 US troops would leave Afghanistan by the end of the year, and an additional 23,000 would leave by 2012. Canada withdrew all its troops in 2011, and other NATO countries pledged to reduce their military presence as well.

In the UK, Prime Minster David Cameron pledged to end British combat operations in Afghanistan by 2015. "I believe the country needs to know there is an end point to all of this," he said, "so from 2015, there will not be troops in anything like the numbers now and, crucially, they will not be in a combat role."

In October 2011, the Afghan government ceased peace talks with the Taliban, two weeks after men claiming to be Taliban representatives killed Afghan peace negotiator, Burhanuddin Rabbani. Two months later, Afghanistan recalled its ambassador from Qatar, protesting attempts to exclude Kabul from US-backed efforts to open a Taliban office there. The US, Germany, and Qatar had been attempting to revive peace talks, and the US reportedly considered transferring Taliban prisoners from Guantanamo Bay in exchange for confidence-building measures from Taliban officials.

2012

After all these years I was home again, standing on the soil of my ancestors. This was the soil on which my great-grandfather had married his third wife, a year before dying in the cholera epidemic that hit Kabul in 1915...it was on this soil that my grandfather had gone on a hunting trip with King Nadir Shah and shot a deer. My mother had died on this soil.

And on this soil, I had fought for my father's love...The kinship I felt suddenly for the old land...it surprised me. I'd been gone long enough to forget and be forgotten. I had a home in a land that might as well be in another galaxy to the people sleeping on the other side of the wall I leaned against. I thought I had forgotten about this land.

But I hadn't. And, under the bony glow of a half-moon, I sensed Afghanistan humming under my feet. Maybe Afghanistan hadn't forgotten me either.

– Khaled Hosseini, *The Kite Runner*

For 2012, summer

"I regretted it at that time, I regret it now and I will always regret it," he says. "But I could not resist, I didn't have a choice because they would have killed me."

– Mirza Hussain, who planted the bombs in the Buddhas of Bamiyan

January 2012: Negotiating with the Taliban

The Taliban announced its plans to open an office in Qatar for peace talks with the US and its allies. This marked the first public step towards negotiations to end the decade-long war in Afghanistan. The Taliban's announcement of its decision to open a liaison office in the Persian Gulf nation could prove to be a watershed, as it was the first time the militant group publicly acknowledged its wish to talk to the US, offering a pathway to do so, former officials and analysts said.

According to news agency reports, US officials, who spoke on condition of anonymity because of the sensitive nature of the subject, said that contacts between the Obama administration and the Afghan Taliban had been secret, limited to preliminary discussions between a few US and Taliban representatives over whether peace talks were even feasible.

The US representatives said that "it would be foolhardy" not to pursue peace talks, however elusive a deal may seem now. "We're going to leave Afghanistan, so it is better to help negotiate an agreement with the Afghan Taliban that would make our exit easier", and help stabilize the country "after we leave," he said.[20]

The Taliban agreed to a preliminary deal, following talks with the Qatari officials and other "relevant parties", to open a liaison office in Qatar. In return, the Taliban asked for the release of its detainees held at the US naval base in Guantanamo Bay, Cuba.

For the first time, President Karzai also agreed to this process, saying "To save Afghanistan from war, from civilian killings, and with the aim to reach peace, Afghanistan agrees to US-Taliban peace negotiations and a liaison office in Qatar for the Taliban." Just a month earlier, in December 2011,

Karzai was quoted as saying that the office in Qatar was not his preference.

The future of the talks could be indefinite due to Pakistan, which harbours most of the Taliban leadership as well as the Haqqani network that is held responsible for major attacks in Kabul. Pakistan believes it should have a say in any talks involving neighbouring Afghanistan, which it fears will develop an alliance with its arch-rival, India. Pakistan has rejected US requests to mount an offensive against the Haqqani network, and relations between the two countries are at an all-time low, following a cross-border incident that resulted in NATO airstrikes killing 24 Pakistani soldiers.

As the United States begins to draw down the nearly 100,000 forces it has in Afghanistan, President Obama's administration wants to use its current extensive military campaign, and an acknowledged but incomplete plan for a long-term American presence in the country, as leverage to draw the Taliban into talks with Karzai representatives.

According to analysts, the likelihood that the Taliban will remain a potent fighting force after most foreign forces leave by the end of 2014, is driving the US and NATO to seek even an incomplete bargain with the insurgents that would keep them talking to the Kabul government.

Back in Afghanistan

Two and a half years since my last visit to Afghanistan, it is 2012 now and I am back in Afghanistan. Winter is here and I land in knee-deep snow and freezing temperatures in the middle of the afternoon on a Saturday.

Since only special vehicles are allowed up to the airport terminal, buses ferry passengers to various parking areas. I was told to go to parking area C, where the car and driver were to meet me. At the parking lot, I struggled to get my bags on a trolley and wheeled it to where I hoped someone would be standing with a piece of paper with my name. No such luck. After waiting for a bit, I got out my iPad, retrieved the email with the driver's number and called. I located them and in ten minutes, we were on our way to the city and my guest house. The driver spoke no English or Urdu but the person accompanying him did and handed me a cell phone with a local sim card.

The streets were bare, the trees leafless, and there was ice everywhere. Vehicles moved slowly. The snow-capped mountains in the distance felt cold but looked stunningly beautiful.

I was booked in a guest house located in the city centre, in Shar-e-naw. At the entrance to the street where the guest house was located, there was a gate and a barricade with several security men with guns. On this street is also a large hotel popular with expats, but there are no names on the buildings or any house numbers. The only sign marking the guest house was a bright blue barricade gate. The guard in my car got off and rang the bell. A man looked through a small gap, which could only accommodate an eye and gave him a 180° view, and then opened the gate for us to enter.

As I was pulling my suitcase, a woman came out, walking briskly towards me and greeted me in Urdu. Taking the suitcase out of my hand, she led me up the stairs, through the front door and turned to the left, into a lobby with a sitting area and a TV, and four doors leading to different rooms. She introduced herself as Najiba and asked me to come down to the basement for some tea once I had settled in. Later, I met the owner of the guest house, Javed, a tall, handsome man with white hair, who welcomed me and promised to set up my wi-fi.

Back upstairs, I unpacked my bags in the 8 x 10 ft. room. The closet was big enough to accommodate all my stuff. I set up the laptop, iPad, and slipped the local sim in my phone. I was starving when dinner was served at 7:00 p.m. There was soup, rice, two vegetables, salad, and a non-vegetarian dish. For dessert, there was fruit and phirni.

As in other guest houses, there were residents from various countries. Since I have a bad memory for names, I repeated them to myself several times: Aziz (Afghan-American from Virginia), Faroukh and Akhbar (Afghan-French), an American whose name I have forgotten, Anoosha (Afghan-American), Frank and Adrienne from Germany, Sarah (an Afghan-Iranian-German), and two Indian men.

Javed jan (as everyone calls him) is an Afghan-German who left Afghanistan when he was 17. He came back in 2002 and set up the guest house on his family property. He has a daughter who is a doctor, married with two children, and lives in the US. The guest house has 40 rooms, and offers both short and long-term stays. Javed also lives in the guest house. Najiba is the manager and supervises and works with about ten other staff.

I am in Kabul to do an assessment of how media covers violence against women. I will be meeting select radio and TV stations. Technically, I am supposed to travel to Jalalabad (on the border of Afghanistan and Pakistan) but considering that the weather is extreme, that might not happen.

On the second day, after meeting my clients and doing my first interview, I go to Finest—a department store with several branches all over Kabul, with the driver and Osman, who is to assist me in my assignment. This particular Finest store is three-storied. I walk around to get a feel of the place, making a mental note of what I might need. Getting a shopping cart, I fill it with dry fruits—walnuts, almonds, raisins, dates, pistachios.

I stop at the cheese counter and get some local Edam, two packets of crackers and apples, kiwis, grapes, and pears. I walk by the coffee counter and see all the 'real coffee' from various places. But I do not have a coffee maker and head to the appliance section on the upper floor. A man working on the floor tells me they do not have a coffee maker, and as I start going back down, I see the line of French presses in five sizes. Ecstatic, I grab the smallest one; turn it upside down to see how much it costs—200 Afs ($4). I can't believe my luck. I dash down to the coffee area and get a tin of Lavazza.

I have a French country knife in the guest house and I buy what will see me through the meals. Back in the guest house, the coffee maker is a big hit and I immediately make friends with die-hard coffee drinkers.

There is more security since I was last here, three years ago. A few months earlier a bomb exploded on Chicken Street. Men are frisked as they enter the street now, but there are shoppers and vendors selling pine nuts and fruit, and beggar women in their full burqas, some with very small children. The shops look a little more prosperous—mostly selling carpets, kilims, wooden antiques (and new ones), jewellery and other items.

In the evenings, we collect at the guest house and like the others times I have been in Afghanistan, it is like a surrogate family. After dinner, Javed jan and some others move over to the pool table and play for several hours. The rest of us hang around and chat, getting to know each other. We talk about our work, home, families, and share stories about Afghanistan.

I offer to cook an Indian meal and it is set for Friday, as there is no dinner in the guest house that night. Najiba and I shop for vegetables, and the menu is dhal, cauliflower, carrots and peas, yogurt raita, rice, and pooris. Fearing it would run short, I hastily made cauliflower soup. The dinner was a hit.

That evening, Faroukh and Akhbar bring out their instruments and we have a music session. They both play the robab and I could see the emotion in their eyes as they played and sang. Faroukh jan is very attached to India and tells me that when he and his family left Afghanistan in the 1970s, they first went to India. Three years later they moved to France. "My wife loves India," he says, dropping some Urdu phrases every now and then. He invites me to his home in France, as does Akhbar jan.

Sometimes when I come back to the guest house, I slip down to the basement for tea. Javed jan is there, reading or listening to music. Come, sit, he says and we begin to chat about his life in Germany and Afghanistan and the future. Najiba jan would also join us, but there was an interesting language barrier. She spoke Urdu and Dari and no English. Javed jan spoke German, French, English, and Dari. Najiba and I became good friends.

There are some changes in Kabul. The city seems to be better managed in terms of water and electricity. In 2006, we ran the genset in the guest house almost all the time. It was shut off at 10:00 p.m. and started at 7:00 a.m. We had coal fuelled bokharis in our rooms. Now, there is better garbage collection; the sidewalks are clean (when they are not covered in snow!). But whether or not things are better in Afghanistan depends on whom you talk to.

I lunch with my friend Omar, whom I have known since 2006. We shared an office at the training centre and have been good friends since. Omar never left Afghanistan and is afraid that the Taliban will return. It is not a good thought. My women friends are equally worried. Under the Taliban, everyone, especially women, really suffered.

Over dinner with Miriam (an Afghan-American) whom I have also known since 2006, I get updated about her life in

Kabul. Miriam is a journalist who grew up in California. She is happy being in Afghanistan, lives by herself, and works for a consulting firm. Marie, my American friend, here since 2004, lives in a house with other people. Her housekeeper, Wasim, helped me in 2009 and is helping me on this trip as well. He tells me of his cousin who was shot at by the Taliban and has been unwell for almost a year now. He may have to bring him to India for some orthopaedic treatment, he says. I offer to help.

Wasim is a colourful man. One of his hobbies is body-building. On the dashboard of his car sits a photograph of him at his body-building best. Too much muscle for me, I turn my eyes away. He tells me a long story of how he got cheated out of being the Mr. Afghanistan No. 1 in a body-building competition last year. It was all rigged, he says in disgust. Never mind, I say, we know you're number one, Wasim jan, you're our number one! He smiles.

I visit Salim, who heads the training centre I was based at in 2006. Over a home-made lunch of kebabs and salad, he tells me something that disturbs me. Salim grew up in Iran and while the Afghans there resembled the locals, once they opened their mouths they gave themselves away because of their accents. So, as children, Salim and his siblings were told not to speak when they went out. I had heard this from my students in 2006 when I asked them what it was like to live there. They also told me that while bread was subsidised for Iranians, it wasn't for them. The life of a refugee is riddled with complications, I thought.

It is time for me to leave. Some friends back in India have asked for *pakols* (the woollen hat worn by many Afghans). Then there is the patu, a large woollen shawl with a delicate border which men drape around them. The day before I leave, Omar comes over with dry fruit gifts. He and Javed get into

My water colour of a man with a pakol

a bit of an argument about what would happen if the Taliban return. Javed has no lived experience of life under the Taliban, Omar has.

As I prepare to leave, I give two of my favourite scarves to Najiba. We hug and promise to see each other soon.

July: Ramadan in Kabul

Six months since my last trip to Afghanistan and I am back in Kabul. It was a hurriedly negotiated assignment, a gender analysis of a large financial project. It is hot and the sun is strong.

This time the living arrangement is different as I live in a house that belongs to a consulting company. The room I am staying in is on the first floor, overlooking the main road; it is large with high windows and an attached bath. There is a writing table, a closet with hangers, and a TV. Down the hall are rooms of two other international consultants, both women, one British, one American. The young Afghan guard on duty at the gate asks if I am from India. We begin to speak in Urdu to each other as I go in and out of the building.

In the next building, there is a common sitting and dining area with a kitchen. Two cooks offer a variety of dishes for about ten people who live in the two houses. The kitchen is well organised as Beth, who has taken on kitchen responsibilities, is a vegetarian (which suits me) and a good organiser. Beth has trained the local cooks to make muesli, cakes, and exotic and healthy bakes for us.

Like many times before, besides reading and writing, my task involves interviewing people. I have been assigned a young Afghan man and woman to work with me. I lose the woman to a consultant who is short-handed. I do not mind as one assistant is enough for my needs. The local consultants make appointments, travel with me to the appointments, and translate, when needed. I check my observations with them and it is always good to have two heads—so much of the work is culturally nuanced.

On this trip, I get to see old friends. Charlotte has worked in Afghanistan for a long time and we meet at Dan's new restaurant. It is more beautiful than the last one. Each of Dan's restaurants has a similar feel—an indoor and outdoor space, lots of local artefacts and kilims. As Charlotte and I catch up over the meal, Dan comes by and insists that we come back one day and have dinner with him. Later, we fix a date and have another enchanted evening under the stars.

This is the first time I have been in Afghanistan during Ramadan. According to government rules, offices and establishments are open from 8:00 a.m. to 1:00 p.m. The fasting requires rest, so it is assumed that not much will get done during this time. When the woman who hired me for the assignment told me this over Skype in Delhi, I dismissed it. How wrong was I. I had to complete my interviews by 1:00 p.m.

During this trip, I have had some uncomfortable discussions with other expats. There is a great deal of complaining about the work culture of Afghans. Once a consultant complained that her local assistant couldn't get the footnotes right. After hearing this three times, I suggested either she supervise it till it is done right or do it herself. I also heard myself say that if the consultancy is so bad, maybe they could look for work in their home countries. I complained that they complained too much. It took them by surprise. Spontaneously, I asked a male consultant: why do you work here? His answer was rather forthright: for the money. This was the first time someone had been so blunt with me. I was disturbed by this, even though I knew it to be true. Next day at breakfast, I asked him if he was serious about what he had said the night before. No, he said with a smile, but it helps to keep the cash coming to keep my family in the style they have got used to!

I have to take a trip to Bamiyan to interview people for my assignment. The male assistant says he can't travel because it is Ramadan and the female assistant, who is pregnant, says her husband does not like her to travel without him. No problem, I said. Mirwais, a young man on leave from school in the US and working in the consulting firm, is designated to travel with me.

As earlier, I take the assignment as another opportunity to visit friends. I call Javed and Najiba jan and they invite me over for dinner. When I reach the guest house, Najiba tells me that Javed had received news that his cousin in the US has died that very morning. He is terribly upset and inconsolable. I offer to cancel dinner and leave after greeting him. No, no, she said, he wants to eat with you.

As the sun goes down, Najiba and I sit out in the yard and catch up. Her mother continues to be in poor health, with multiple complications such as diabetes, high blood pressure, and arthritis. Her brother and his family, Najiba, another sister, and her mother all live together. The brother has a drinking problem and there are instances of violence in the home. Najiba is upset by all this. Close to forty, there is pressure on her to marry as well.

Relationships, like anywhere in the world, are complicated. More so, in Afghanistan.

My friend Omar got married last year to a relative on the mother's side of the family. In 2006, when he was in his late 20s, I asked how come he was still single. He told me he lived with his widowed mother and wanted someone who could take care of her. I told him a wife is a companion, not a caretaker for a mother. I know, he said, but what do I do about my mother? Hire a maid who will also serve as a companion to her, I told him. A few years later, Omar married a woman ten years younger than him and rapidly had two children. His wife's family is good to him and he is settled and happy, it seems. He continues to be a good friend.

Several married Afghan women friends have difficult lives. Because they are prominent in women's rights movements, their husbands do not want them to be seen on TV, speaking out on injustices against women and girls. One husband threatened to take his life unless his wife promised not to appear on TV. Another, after the couple divorced, continued to blackmail and threaten her, spread lies and slandered her, even when she was posted in another country. A member of parliament, whose husband divorced her, is bitter and angry almost all the time—she cannot forgive him for leaving her for a younger woman.

Most married Afghan men I have met seem, at least on the surface, to have a fairly calm family life. But that is true of men almost all over the world; it is women who pay a high price for wanting a life—in or outside the home.

In 2002, right after the fall of the Taliban, Norwegian journalist Åsne Seierstad spent months in the home of a bookstore owner, Shah Muhammad Rais, and wrote the best-seller, The Bookseller of Kabul. The book was a portrayal of Rais's family, his marriages, and children. When the book was released, Rais flew to Norway and filed a suit against Seierstad, claiming her account was false as she had manipulated the information under his hospitality. The suit was settled in her favour in 2011.

Seierstad, commenting on the decision said, "The book came after the fall of the Taliban; it says something about Afghan family life. Those kinds of stories—what happens behind the scenes on a TV screen—are important." The fact that her subjects were not at ease with the manner in which they were portrayed was not "ideal", she added, but she was confident that she had presented the family in a "respectful" way. "I have admiration for [Rais] and the fact that he continued to sell his books. He is an Afghan hero and I think I portrayed that, but he is also an Afghan patriarch. Journalism is about going out and making choices. It is my book, it is my decision."

I read The Bookseller of Kabul after my first trip in 2004. It described the family so fully and gave a piercing insight into their lives. I met Rais's son in 2004 and, on almost every trip I made to Afghanistan, visited their bookshop. I discussed the book with my expat friends. Some felt Seierstad violated Rais's hospitality, but that is not really the question, is it? How accurate is the book in its portrayal of their life, I would argue, is the real question. Every book is written through the eyes of the writer. As I read it, I felt there was no judgement, just reportage of what Åsne saw and observed. But then, no one really knows what she actually saw.

In Bamiyan and Band-e-Amir

In Kabul, when Omar and I meet at Wakhan Café, I tell him I am excited about going to Bamiyan. He tells me to stay at the Silk Road Hotel. As luck would have it, the office has already booked Mirwais and me there. When we touch down at the Bamiyan gravel airstrip, Abdul, the driver from the hotel, is waiting for us.

Buddhas of Bamiyan—view from my hotel window

We reach the hotel in about 20 minutes after a ride through streets with poplar trees, mud architecture and clear skies. The hotel is a concrete two-storied building, looking out into the Bamiyan Buddha caves. In the garden, roses are blooming.

In 2001, when the Taliban were at the height of their power in Afghanistan, Taliban leader Mullah Omar waged a war against idolatry. The Taliban bombed and took down two standing Buddhist statues. Once the largest in the world—one measured 53 metres in height—they were carved into the sandstone cliff face of the Bamiyan valley during the sixth century. The destruction of Bamiyan Buddhas led to global condemnation of the Taliban regime.

Our hotel is owned by a Japanese journalist, Hiromi, and her Afghan husband. Over the years, they have built a successful business. The food is healthy and includes delicious Japanese cuisine (one of my favourites). Hiromi runs a boutique full of

Hiromi's map of Bamiyan

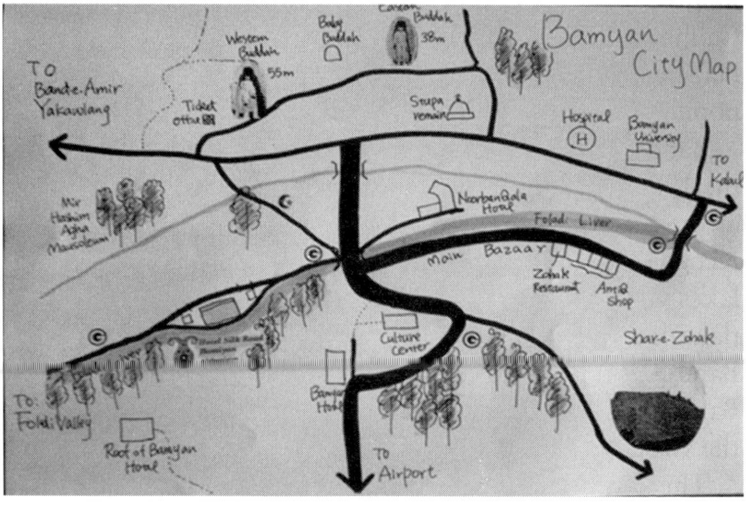

handmade scarves, sweaters, bags, clothes sourced from local communities and other places. She is clearly multi-talented and has made a map of Bamiyan which is on the wall. (European Synchrotron Radiation Facility, March 24, 2011.)

The Band-e-Amir

In the afternoon, Mirwais, Abdul, and I set off for a drive to Band-e-Amir, a collection of lakes west of the famous Buddhas of Bamiyan. We drove about 75 kms from Bamiyan, close to the town of Yalawang. The drive from Bamiyan to Yalawang was on a recently completed highway, financed by the Japanese.

In two hours, with the rugged Hindu Kush mountains in the backdrop, we reached the most spectacular expanse of blue water I had ever seen. The Band-e-Amir is a national park with lakes separated by natural dams made of travertine—a form of limestone deposited by mineral springs, especially hot springs. Band-e-Amir literally means 'commander's dam', a reference to Imam Ali, the first Imam of the Shia Muslims and the fourth Caliph of the Sunni Muslims. The area is dominated by ethnic Hazaras, who make up around nine per cent of Afghanistan's population, and are followers of Shia Islam.

Band-e-Amir was supposed to be the first national park in the 1960s, but due to the instability of the Kabul government at the time, that did not happen. However, in 2009, it was recognised as a world heritage site. It is made up of six principal lakes which have rather charming names: Band-e Gholaman (lake of the slaves); Band-e Qambar (lake of Caliph Ali's slave); Band-e Haibat (grandiose lake); Band-e Panir (lake of cheese); Band-e Pudina (lake of wild mint); Band-e Zulfiqar (lake of the sword of Ali).

The Band-e Haibat is the biggest and deepest of the

lakes, with an average depth of approximately 150 metres. Abdul, Mirwais, and I hovered around the top of Band-e Haibat, admired the view, took photos, and then headed back to the car.

Bamiyan and the Buddhas

Bamiyan lies about 240 kms north-west of Kabul and was the site of an early Hindu–Buddhist monastery from which Bamiyan takes its name (Sanskrit *varmayana*, "coloured").

The Bamiyan valley marked the westerly-most point of Buddhist expansion and was a crucial hub of trade for much of the last millennium. It was a place where east met west, and its archaeology reveals a blend of Greek, Turkish, Persian, Chinese, and Indian influences, found nowhere else in the world.

Situated on the ancient Silk Route, the town was a key location as all trade between China and the Middle East passed through it. The Hunas made it their capital in the fifth century. The Shar-i-Zohak mound, ten miles south of the valley, is the site of a citadel that guarded the city, and the ruins of an acropolis were found there as recently as the 1990s.

Many statues of the Buddha were carved on the sides of the cliffs facing Bamiyan city. Three colossal statues were carved 4,000 ft. apart on the cliff face of a mountain. One of them was 175 ft. (53 m) high standing statue of Buddha, the world's tallest. According to sources, the ancient statue was carved during the Kushan period in the fifth century. It is said that at one time, two thousand monks meditated in caves among the sandstone cliffs.

Further enhancing the cultural capital of the city, the oldest oil painting was discovered in Bamiyan in 2008 in the caves behind the partially destroyed colossal statues. Scientists from the European Synchrotron Radiation Facility have confirmed that the oil paintings, probably of either walnut or poppy seed oil, are present in 12 of the 50 caves dating from the fifth to ninth centuries. The murals typically have a white base layer of a lead compound, followed by an upper layer of natural or artificial pigments mixed with either resins or walnut or poppy seed drying oils. Possibly, the paintings may be the work of artists who travelled on the Silk Road.

The caves at the base of these statues were used by the Taliban for storing weapons. After the Taliban were driven from the region, civilians made their homes in the caves. Recently, Afghan refugees escaped the persecution of the Taliban regime by hiding in these caves. These refugees discovered a fantastic collection of Buddhist statues as well as jars holding more than ten thousand fragments of ancient Buddhist manuscripts, a large part of which is now included in the Schøyen Collection.

The Schøyen Collection is the largest private manuscript collection in the world, located mostly in Oslo and London. Formed in the 20th century by Martin Schøyen, it comprises manuscripts of global provenance, spanning 5,000 years of history. It contains more than 13,000 manuscript items; the oldest book is about 5,300 years old. There are manuscripts from 134 different countries and territories, representing 120 distinct languages. This discovery from Bamiyan has created a sensation among scholars, and the find has been compared with the discovery of the Dead Sea scrolls.

Bamiyan, a small town with a bazaar at its centre, has no infrastructure in terms of electricity, gas, or water supplies. For decades, it has been the centre of combat between zealous Taliban forces and the anti-Taliban alliance—mainly Hizb-i-Wahdat—amid clashes among the warlords of local militia.

Mirwais, Abdul, and I walk down the one-road market, looking at the shops with local goods. My interest is the antique shop which Abdul directs us to. It is called shop number 368. The shopkeeper is kind and opens up the rugs and kilims for me. Mirwais and Abdul admire the jewellery. I buy three rugs and some jewellery, including rings for Abdul and Mirwais.

We drive out to the Women's Garden, a space organised by the NGO, Parsa. Besides the Garden, there is a small guest house with a restaurant and a beautiful garden with flowers, vegetables, and stunning poplars.

We order lunch and, while it is being prepared, walk around the garden. Mirwais and I take photographs. We then sit under the poplar trees and listen to Abdul's story. He points out—in the distance—to where he was shot by the Taliban and narrowly escaped. He tells us about his family and his job as a driver which is only for the non-winter months in Bamiyan. The hotel closes down as Hiromi moves to Kabul to avoid the very bitter winter.

2012–2013: The continuing war and insurgency

The insurgency and war in Afghanistan continue. Many observers now believe that future peace in Afghanistan can only come if the government in Kabul negotiates with the Taliban. According to news agency reports, the Taliban announcement to open an office in Qatar in June 2013 was seen as a positive step in those negotiations, but mistrust on both sides remained high. Hopes for peace talks were equally high early in 2012 before the Taliban in Afghanistan announced, in a strongly-worded statement in March of that year, that they were suspending preliminary peace negotiations with the US.

There have been numerous Taliban attacks on Kabul in the

past two years and, in September 2012, the group carried out a high profile raid on NATO's Camp Bastion base. In the same month, the US military handed over control of the controversial Bagram prison—housing more than 3,000 Taliban fighters and terrorism suspects—to the Afghan authorities.

In recent years, the Taliban have also relied relied increasingly on roadside bombs as a means of fighting NATO and Afghan forces. The exact number of people killed by these bombs is difficult to calculate, but the interior ministry says they were responsible for killing most of the 1,800 Afghan national police personnel who died in 2012. During the same time period, estimates suggest, about 900 Afghan National Army soldiers were killed by roadside bombs.

In August 2013, the Afghan government-backed High Peace Council opposed "tough pre-conditions" for talks with the Taliban and urged the government and the Taliban to show flexibility in order to bring the stalled Qatar process back on track.

The remarks came weeks after the closure of the Taliban office in Qatar, following a row with the Afghan government over the use of the flag, and a plaque bearing the name of the Islamic Emirate of Afghanistan—the name the Taliban used when they were in power.

President Hamid Karzai refused to send the peace council members to Qatar as he considered that the flag and the plaque promoted the office as an embassy of a government-in-exile. The Taliban closed the office following the Qatari officials' decision to lower the flag and remove the signboard of the Islamic Emirate. The top Taliban leadership said they would not talk in Qatar until they were allowed to display the flag and plaque at the office once again, a Taliban official told *The Express Tribune*.

In order to revive the dialogue process, the Afghan High Peace Council called upon the Afghan government and the Taliban to give up these conditions before the talks begin. They mentioned they were in touch with Pakistan and it wanted to free all Taliban prisoners, including (Mullah Omar's deputy) Mullah Abdul Ghani Baradar.

Afghans attached high hopes to the visit of the Afghan President, Hamid Karzai to Islamabad, as the talks could help in the reconciliation process. The Afghan government is aware and openly says that Pakistan has a key role in the Afghan peace process. The Taliban leadership is based in Pakistan, and the Afghans want it to extend support to the peace process and facilitate direct contact between the peace council and authorised Taliban representatives. They also want Pakistan to provide safe passage to Taliban leaders who are prepared to engage the Afghan government in direct negotiations.

In the meanwhile, Afghanistan continued to face challenges due to the conflict. In 2012, according to official statistics, 94,299 Afghans had been internally displaced by conflict and 32,490 of them were living in the 55 Kabul informal settlements; 9,851 people were newly registered as internally displaced. This figure increased substantially in 2013—a total of 502,628 Afghans were internally displaced by conflict and 2.5 million registered Afghans were forced to move to neighbouring countries.[21]

War, displacement and migration bring—besides the physical suffering—an accompanying burden of mental challenges, which are often ignored. In October 2013, Joel Brinkley, professor of journalism at Stanford University and former foreign correspondent for *The New York Times*, reported that Afghan soldiers shot and killed at least 135 of the American servicemen who were training them over the past five years. In

2012, the United States Agency for International Development interviewed large numbers of young people in Afghanistan and found them generally to be "disenfranchised, unskilled, uneducated, and neglected". These people, it added, "are most susceptible to joining the insurgency".

But, says Brinkley, multiple medical studies over the past nine years indicate that these disaffected young people are less likely to volunteer for the insurgency than they are to join the tens of millions of Afghans who suffer from post-traumatic stress disorder, clinical depression, perpetual deep anxiety, and other debilitating trauma-related mental illnesses that are rife in the country. And these mental illnesses can sometimes lead to irrational, violent acts—like killing your trainers.

This trauma, Brinkley argues, could be thoroughly undercutting the strategies of the United States and its allies in Afghanistan, even as western forces are leaving. But the American military and policy-making community was not even aware of the problem, therefore little was being done to address it or compensate for it.

Brinkley interviewed Air Force Col. Erik Goepner who, when stationed in Afghanistan, said he learnt that these environmental factors can lead to severe mental illness—even though to this day, American servicemen receive no training on psychological issues before leaving for Afghanistan. "As an American military commander, you want to win," Goepner noted in the interview. To him, it was clear that even after a decade of warfare, there was to be no "decisive win. And so you look back and ask: Why isn't it going the way I want it to?"

In part, to help find the answer, Goepner began working "with a lot of Afghans" and came away with "the idea that something was going on in the mental head space". Psychology was not among his areas of expertise but, over time, he read a number of psychological studies and learnt that more than half of Afghans suffer from clinical PTSD. And in some studies, the number afflicted with severe anxiety and clinical depression exceeded 70 per cent.[22]

American political and military leaders never talked about this as part of the challenges they face in Afghanistan. In fact, said Paul Pillar, who was the CIA's national intelligence officer for the Near East and South Asia for several years, "I do not have any recollection of that; I do not recall seeing any reports on that."

Denial is not only the purview of the Americans and military leaders. Social scientist Anna Maria Cardinalli, who worked for the military in Afghanistan for several months, points out how average Afghans greet visitors with "a vacant and unsettled stare in the eyes". Cardinalli was the lead researcher for a Pentagon study on paedophilia in Afghanistan. Over generations, older men have taken tens of thousands of little boys as lovers, an Afghan custom, often leaving the boys with severe emotional, and perhaps even physical, wounds. The children remain untreated because mental health care is virtually non-existent, and parents are generally ashamed to seek treatment for physical wounds.

Boys, girls, teenagers, adult men and women, and the elderly—all are beaten down, battered, and bruised. The years of war ripped apart not just the physical infrastructure, the psychological structure of Afghan society has also been devastated.

All of this adds to the toxic mix of dysfunction. One critical result of this is that most Afghan civilians want nothing at all to do with the Afghan government or the western military forces supporting it—even though their support "is the critical element" of counter-insurgency strategy, says Col. Erik Goepner.

2013

"In May 2013, we held one of the first National Youth Debates with over 500 young Afghans asking for government accountability around the peace process. The final message from every young Afghan was, 'listen to our voices before the insurgents recruit us'."

– Wazhma Frogh, civil society leader and women's rights activist

December 2013: Learning from civil society

A year and a half later, I am back in Afghanistan. I have been invited by an NGO to meet with diverse groups to talk about civil society in India, along with women from Azerbaijan and Pakistan. It is winter and cold, but there is no snow, as there was in January 2012.

Driving through the city, I see changes. There is more greenery, the sidewalks are cleaner, and some of the side roads have been tarred. The driver of the car pulls into a building opposite the Turkish embassy, with its usual security and multiple gates. It is the Kabul Star Hotel, where I am booked for this stay. Upon checking in, I am given the Internet password and a key to my room, overlooking the street, on the 5th floor.

This is the first time I am staying at a hotel in Kabul, and it feels a little strange. By 7:00 p.m., I am hungry and order room service which comes 90 minutes later, after two reminders. There was some mix-up, I am told and I can understand how this could happen. I am especially pleased to see women behind the reception desk, working alongside men.

Breakfast is self-service—hot and cold cereals, eggs, toast, naan, apples, juices, tea, and instant coffee. Khalisa, from Azerbaijan, and I take a table near the window and through the vertical blinds we can see the sun and the blue sky. Aziz, our host, tells us that Fatima, the Pakistani woman, could not join us today but would be in Kabul tomorrow.

We travel to the offices of an umbrella organisation of NGOs near a school and enter a bokhari-heated room where members of the steering committee were sitting. Other members come in slowly and after a full round of introductions, we started. The committee described their work to us, highlighting the challenges of bringing together different civil society groups, including youth and women. There are also issues of funding, and security. Khalisa and I talked about similar challenges in our countries.

We moved to Bagh-e-Babur, or Babur's garden, and were joined by another fifteen CSO representatives. We were running short of time and as the discussion was in English and Dari, translation back and forth also took some time. After the group left, we were invited to a cup of tea on the veranda of the building, and one of the Afghan women told Khalisa that she did not have to cover her head if she did not want to. Whatever makes you comfortable, she said. Khalisa lowered her scarf, revealing a thick mass of dark curly hair.

We strolled on the grounds and were sad that the entry door to Babur's tomb was locked. As it started to get cooler, we headed out of the Bagh-e-Babur and went back to the hotel.

Khalisa and I agreed to meet at 7:00 p.m. for dinner. The dining hall at the hotel was large, with a mezzanine full of local people. There was live music and we chose to sit at the table closest to the singers, who sang heart-warming ghazals.

Khalisa and I chatted. I learned about women's groups in Azerbaijan and her own career as an activist, and discovered that she had even run for parliament as an independent candidate.

The next day at breakfast Fatima joined us and told us stories of her trip to Turkey, right before she came to Kabul. We visited the offices of the High Peace Council in a large and very cold building. Fatima shared her experiences in Pakistan and the Swat valley of de-radicalization and reintegration of young men and families who had been working with the insurgents. It seemed that similar work was being done by the HPC in Afghanistan.

Everyone seemed to be in a hurry. We hurried off to

parliament to meet 12 MPs and hear their views on the contribution CSOs can make to the new Afghanistan and the cause of nation building. Over lunch, there was a discussion about insurgency and violence against women against the backdrop of the general violence in society.

After this, we rushed over to the Afghan Women's Skill Development Centre (AWSDC) shelter to meet around 40 women. I told them how impressed I had been with my visit to the Centre last year. Indian NGOs have a hard time managing shelter homes for women as the state-run homes are in bad shape and women do not really seek shelter in them.

Things seem to be improving but so much more is needed—money, facilities, capacity building, and exposure. For example, there could be more women's shelters, maybe several in each province. I think about the situation in India, and almost any other country, where there is paucity of adequate shelters for women and children who face violence.

We visited the Afghan Women's Network (AWN), a network of women's organisations and individuals. I know several of the men and women who come into the meeting room and we greet each other over tea and biscuits. After a round of introductions, the three of us made presentations. As it was a women's network, I talked about the kind of laws and policies adopted in India in recent times, institutional mechanisms, and the role of women's organisations in enabling and facilitating this. I talked about our challenges and failures in implementing laws and policies, and the lack of coordinated action on the part of women's organisations on critical issues.

Khalisa spoke about the gains in Azerbaijan and the importance of education for women. Fatima talked about solidarity and how her organisation has attempted to do that on women's issues in South Asia.

The exchange trip raised many questions. What can CSOs do about development in Afghanistan? What has been the record of CSOs in Azerbaijan, India, and Pakistan?

Civil society organisations are not entirely new to Afghanistan. They existed as far back as the 1990s when the Agency Coordinating Body for Afghan Relief (ACBAR) coordinated the work of NGOs in the refugee camps of Peshawar. The number of networks grew post-2001, with specialised networks becoming more prominent (such as the Afghan Women's Network for women's rights organisations).

A 2012 study conducted by Altai Consulting says that civil society actors who were interviewed, complained about the lack of coordination among networks themselves and their inability to truly represent those whom they claim to be representing. Like the NGOs themselves, the networks could also be classified in two ways: donor-backed and formalised institutions such as AWN and ACBAR; and those that have emerged through an informal grassroots process.[23]

For example, the Mazar Civil Society Union was created by a number of NGO heads who wished to make a distinction between actual NGOs and CSOs, and construction companies or political organisations that had registered as NGOs/CSOs in order to take advantage of tax breaks. Once they managed to make the separation, their initial aim gave way to a bigger objective of coordinating the work of civil society organisations, to increase the impact of assistance and exert pressure on the government. The Union has not registered itself with any governmental body (although all the individual NGOs represented are registered), and remains an informal grassroots movement that is visibly very active.

There have been, and are, traditional civil society structures, such as various forms of village and elder councils in certain parts of Afghanistan. They have been active in acting as a bridge between the people and the government, building consensus on issues of common concern, and resolving disputes at the community level. However, such bodies typically remain fairly local and assemble on geographic and tribal lines. In recent years, councils have been developed based on these traditional councils and this has blurred the geographic and tribal lines.

Traditional bodies are starting to play different roles in Afghan communities. For example, beyond traditional elders' shuras at the community level (which generally facilitate dispute resolution), the National Solidarity Program (NSP) set up a network of community development councils (CDCs) at the village level to implement development grants from the ministry of rural rehabilitation and development (MRRD). They receive requests for development projects from the community and present them to the government. In this way, they liaise between the community and their elected representatives. The MRRD has established district development assemblies (DDAs) to coordinate the work of CDCs at the district level. Officially, each CDC in the district sends a representative to the district assembly; however, in practice, their scope and level of activity is limited.

In 2009, the Independent Directorate for Local Governance (IDLG) launched the Afghan Social Outreach Program (ASOP), which formed ASOP shuras that are active in a number of Afghan districts, in an attempt to involve local traditional authorities in governmental processes. In many Afghan districts, ASOP shuras co-habit with DDAs and other sector specific councils.

Currently, the role of traditional councils remains primarily one of dispute resolution and of linking the community with the government. It has also been found that, at the community level, it is not uncommon for community members to seek advice from their elder councils.

The CDCs established by NSP differ from traditional councils in a number of important respects: CDCs are elected bodies whereas traditional councils are not; CDCs have been established across the entire country, whereas traditional councils do not exist everywhere. Women have been included in CDCs and the membership terms, duration of office, and terms of reference of CDC members are fixed by the NSP.

Some CSOs in the sample did maintain linkages with traditional councils, as a means of anchoring themselves in the community and increasing their legitimacy in the eyes of the community, although it seems that this opportunity is not capitalised enough by the civil society sector.

Catching up with friends

I have a coffee meeting with Omar. At the Flower Street Coffee Shop, we choose to sit in the yard under an umbrella partially shading us from the sun. We catch up on his work, the developments in his organisation and changes in the staff and policy direction. Like many NGOs, his lives from one project to another. When one project dries up, others come in. I ask if there is anxiety about the elections next year—2014—and the NATO troops moving out. No, says Omar, I think we will be okay. Omar still dreams of getting a master's degree and tells me of his attempt to get a scholarship to the UK. He did everything well but did not secure the marks needed in his English exam. He hopes to travel to Delhi, attend a two-week coaching class and then retake the test. He says he is stagnating, needs a change, and a higher qualification means better work prospects.

We talk about my Kabul book and what it contains. I'd like him to read a few of the chapters and give feedback. Sure, he says, sharing the story of a friend who wrote about a radio station owner in Herat and their drinking together. Omar suggested to his friend to remove those sections from the book as it could have implications for the person he was referring to. We talk about different cultural sensibilities.

Omar tells me he would like me to taste the grapes on his family farm. In the summer, there is a bumper harvest. I suggest they make wine. He laughs. I know wine making is not possible in Afghanistan today. I ask what they do with the surplus. We make a drink, he says, describing the process of extracting the juice of the grapes, adding apples and cooking it overnight.

My lunch appointment does not show up as she has been locked down due to a demonstration on the Jalalabad Road, so I eat by myself. Despite it being Saturday and a holiday in Kabul, the Serena is quiet and there is an air of sadness around, unlike the 2006 days when it was lively and full of action. The next day, I leave quietly.

2014

"People say the country is going to collapse, but I don't believe it, Afghans are too strong for it [to happen]. Now one of the differences is that young people are speaking out. Now they have found their voices. It's the same with the women."

– Nancy Hatch Dupree, resident of Kabul since 1962, known as the "Grandmother of Kabul."

2014: An election year

An election year and the first time in Afghanistan's history that power will be democratically transferred.

In July 2013, parliament passed a set of election laws considered crucial to holding the election on time. The first law laid out the composition and rules for Afghanistan's election commission and another commission to adjudicate complaints about voter fraud and other irregularities. The second law stipulated how the voting would be held.

Presidential elections were held in Afghanistan on April 5 with a second round on June 14. Incumbent President Hamid Karzai was not eligible to run, having had two five year terms. The registration period for presidential nominations was open from September 16, 2013 until October 6, 2013.

A total of 27 candidates were confirmed to be running for office. However, on October 22, Afghanistan's independent election commission disqualified sixteen of the candidates, leaving only eleven in the race. By April 2014, three candidates gave up the race and decided to support some of the eight remaining candidates. Opinion polls showed Abdullah Abdullah and Ashraf Ghani as the front-runners. The first round of voting had Abdullah in the lead. There were reports of polling sites running out of ballot papers due to a high turnout.

Pakistan sealed its border with Afghanistan during the electoral period in order to reduce the chances of cross-border attacks.

The results of the second round would determine the new leader of Afghanistan; results came in after the run-off on June 14, two months after the first round. Preliminary results were expected on July 2 and the final result on July 22. However, widespread accusations of fraud delayed the announcement; in September 2014, the independent election commission named Ashraf Ghani the winner.

The six months from April to September were a time of great uncertainty in Afghanistan. Afghans waited eagerly for a new government in the hope of new direction and better governance. There was anxiety about Abdullah Abdullah's claim that there was fraud in the second round, in which he lost to Ashraf Ghani. Outside Afghanistan, many countries held their breath as much was at stake. An important factor was the withdrawal of American and NATO troops that, so far, had contained insurgency within the country.

In May 2014, President Barack Obama announced that US combat operations in Afghanistan would end in December 2014. A residual force of 9,800 troops would remain in the country, training Afghan security forces and supporting counter-terrorism operations against remnants of Al-Qaeda. This force would be halved by the end of 2015, and consolidated at Bagram Air Base and Kabul. Obama also announced that all US forces, with the exception of a "normal embassy presence", would be removed from Afghanistan by the end of 2016. These plans were confirmed with the signing of the bilateral security agreement between the United States and Afghanistan on September 30, 2014.[24]

But the threat of terrorism and insurgency continued. To combat this, the Special Operations Joint Task Force—Afghanistan, the remnant US/NATO special forces organisation—included a counter-terrorism unit. According to the US Special Operations Command Fact Book for 2015, this unit was to conduct offensive operations in Afghanistan to degrade the Taliban, Al-Qaeda, and the Haqqani networks to prevent them from establishing operationally significant safe havens "which threaten the stability and sovereignty of the government of the Islamic Republic of Afghanistan and the United States".

Meanwhile, on September 21, presidential candidates Ashraf Ghani and Abdullah Abdullah signed an agreement for power sharing in Kabul. In a televised ceremony, they signed the documents, shook hands and embraced. Ghani would be the president and Abdullah the chief executive officer (CEO) with powers equal to a prime minister in the traditional sense.

According to Mujib Mashal, writing in *Al Jazeera*, Ghani and Abdullah are products of two different schools of thought, with divergent trajectories. Yet, the two men's attempts in the last years of Karzai's presidency to rebrand themselves, combined with the responsibility they shouldered now, have brought them to a shared reality. And there, perhaps, lies the explanation for how the two leaders have quickly put much of the bitterness of the elections behind them. Gen. John Campbell, the commander of the US and international forces in Afghanistan, believes Ghani's skills and expertise complement Abdullah's, and vice versa. What unites them is a common understanding of the grave risks the country faces and a realistic outlook on the country's dependence on the West.[25]

While Karzai stubbornly refused to sign the bilateral agreement with the US, the two men have embraced the foreign presence, and have even asked for a reconsideration of the withdrawal schedule. (Approximately 5,500 US troops are currently slated to remain in Afghanistan beyond the end of the year, and the White House is reportedly examining an adjustment to that plan.) "We are in a much better place with them than we were with Karzai," said Campbell.

While many, in and out of Afghanistan, questioned the lack of transparency in this power sharing arrangement between Ghani and Abdullah, I was relieved. Since April, the country has been almost in limbo due to the elections and then the vote recounting. In the meanwhile, the insurgency and attacks on various government officials, buildings and civilians continued, causing great damage and losses to the country and people.

Winter in Kabul

It is November of 2014 and, almost one year later, I am back in Afghanistan. There is a new government and I am curious to see what the mood is.

I am staying at the same guest house I stayed at in January 2012, owned and managed by Javed and Najiba. This time, I was the only guest for a week and had an entire floor to myself. I suggested that the cook be asked not to come in only for us, so we all cooked, enjoying each other's company in the kitchen and each making different dishes. Javed is a salad specialist, Najiba does the pulao and kormas. I do the pastas and soups. Our interactions are innovative too. Javed and I speak to each other in English, Najiba, who grew up in Pakistan, and I speak in Hindi. There is a lot of translation back and forth.

I ask Javed jan what has changed since the new government was sworn-in two months ago. Not much, he says, things move slowly here, you know how it is. Yes, I do, I say. But they can be better, quite easily, if the government was not interested in only making money and had some specialist do the job, says Javed. Several of Javed jan's friends drop by during the long cold evenings and there is talk around the bokhari. Sometimes, I join them. Despite the gloom-and-doom news that surrounds us, many of these people are entrepreneurs and have invested rather heavily in Afghanistan. Having lived out of the country, they are keen to come back and make a difference. They have money to invest, an education, and a deep love for their country.

I requested a sunny room and was given a south-facing one on the first floor with windows on two sides. There are still some leaves on the trees. The temperature is about eight degrees in the day and below three degrees at night. The air is crisp, the sky is blue and the sun shines brightly. The birds chirp and I feel content. The guest house has grape vines and many chinar (maple) trees. There are geraniums, snapdragons and basil, which are on their last legs, due to the changing weather. There is a swing, which has been retired for the winter.

I am here for a month to work with the Afghan Women's Network, assisting them in developing a three-year strategic plan. The AWN is a network of women's organisations and individuals that also organised the 5 Million Women Campaign in 2009. They have cleared a desk for me in a room that I share with two other women, who work in the advocacy section.

This week I have met some old friends and made new ones. I look forward to catching up with my Afghan friends, hearing about their lives, and getting an insight into how they see things unfolding in their country. The expat friends have a slightly different view of what is going on, as is to be expected. I have observed the number of expats dwindling over the years, primarily due to violence. Those who are here, live in highly secure compounds and are isolated from the rest of the local people. This almost forced isolation is a shame as they miss a great deal.

On Friday, Osman came to meet me with his cousin and we went to his friends' restaurant on the airport road. In 2006, when I was training journalists in Kabul, Osman was my guide—driving me around, taking me to markets and restaurants, and teaching me Dari. Eight years later, Osman has filled out, wears a salwar kurta and waistcoat, and looks prosperous. We sat out in the small patch of green in front of the restaurant, with the traffic buzzing. We chatted over elaichi chai, pistachios, chana, raisins, savouries, and toffees.

What are you doing these days, I ask Osman. I am a journalist Anita jan, he says, smiling. Really, I say. How did this happen? He tells me that he worked as a fixer with several British journalists, travelling with them, and acting as a translator. I picked up writing from them, he says. As the security situation worsened, the journalists left and he took over their role. He writes under a pseudonym for various British media. "I can get all kinds of information that foreign journalists can't," he boasts, "but I can't write under my real name as I'd get killed," gesturing with his hand across his throat.

We talk about Afghanistan—its state of affairs, the new government, the Taliban, and the role of the US, NATO, and the increasing insurgency. Osman, like many other Afghans, can't afford to do just one thing. He tells me he has a construction business and points to the pink and white three-storey house that he had rented out to a security company. He also does logistics and security, and the cousin at our table works with him. In Afghanistan, like the rest of the region, people tend to trust family members while doing business. He says he wants to move out of the construction business as there is too much investment upfront. But when the money comes in, it is a lot.

Osman tells me that there is future in the stone and marble business. He started dealing with an investor in Dubai, supplying him with the raw material which would go through Iran to Dubai, where it is polished and then sold to clients in the US and Europe. However, this means that he has to deal with the Taliban, as the raw materials are in an area under their control. I do not negotiate with them, he says, others do.

Osman is a serious conspiracy theory man. He talks about

the 'game' or conspiracy between the US, Iran, Pakistan, and the Afghan government. He says that he has seen first-hand the attacks on Afghans, how the Americans covered them up and the media stayed silent. It is the way things are in our part of the world, I say. Osman is angry, very angry, and says that between America and Pakistan, Afghanistan is screwed. This is a commonly held view among many Afghans I meet. They lay the blame for the state of their country squarely on Pakistan, Russia and the US, often in that order.

That evening I visit a German colleague who has been in Kabul for almost three years. To reach her home, I call for a cab from Kabul Kar and seventeen-year old Waseeb appears, with a fashionable haircut. How is business, I ask him. Not so good, he says. Their cars and drivers have been reduced greatly. There isn't much demand as there are fewer expats and consultants coming in, even for short-term assignments. Many guest houses have closed down and those that continue to function have low occupancy. "I also run a guest house and can give you a room for half the price you are paying currently," he says. "Maybe you could suggest my guest house to your Indian friends?" Maybe, I say.

Waseeb tells me there will be more unemployment as foreign contractors and organisations wind up and leave. How will all these people be absorbed, I wonder? I share this with my German friend and she confirms that things are indeed very different and difficult. Lives of the expats have changed. Gone are the days of going out at night after work and on weekends, meeting in restaurants and hanging out. Embassies and organisations stick to their own. There is not that much interaction and that is a shame, she says. Her home has a garden with roses and we sit on the veranda with tea and

Turkish sweets. Her husband is originally from Turkey but grew up in Germany. He works as a journalist but was not able to get much work in Afghanistan. In two months, they will leave for Germany.

Since I came to Kabul, there have been four insurgency attacks. Some people have died, others injured, and there has been substantial loss of property. People have high expectations of the new Ghani government, yet there is concern about growing unemployment, rising prices, and anxiety about the majority of NATO and American forces leaving Afghanistan. People can see the rise of the Taliban and are afraid, as we all should be.

Riding with Fahim

Every morning at around 9:00 a.m. my phone rings and Fahim, the driver at AWN, tells me he is in front of my guest house. He calls out a hearty, "Hello Anita jan, good morning" every time. We both marvel at the beauty of the November days, with clear blue skies, bright sun, and cool weather.

Fahim speaks some Urdu which makes it easy for us to communicate. He knows Urdu from his time in Pakistan, and his greatest pleasure is to turn on the radio station that plays Hindi film music. Since the songs are mostly from the '60s and the '70s, I know them well. We sing along, laughing at the lyrics, which are usually about love won and lost.

This morning he played a song whose lyrics, roughly translated, would mean: how full of grief is life; it kills me and it kills you. So, let us get together and kill grief. I pretend to have a knife in my hand, and stab and kill grief. We laugh hysterically, stopping only when the speed-breaker jolts us out of our mirth.

Yesterday, I stopped to do an errand and when I got back into the car, Fahim was chatting with his sister in California. "This is Anita jan from Delhi, and she speaks Urdu," he said. His sister and I waved to each other and chatted for a few minutes before the phone fell from his hands as he was driving. He said he had a brother in London and two more in Afghanistan.

Later, driving me home from work, he showed me a picture of his seven-year old son. How many children, I asked? Four, he said. It is time to stop, I said, never taking off my family planning hat. Yes, he said, stop! He asked me how many children I had. One, I said, a son. Really, he asked, no daughter? Now, in India this would not even be a question! I am enjoying my time with Fahim jan. Thanks to his good nature, we start and end the day in good spirits.

Driving through Shahrara

There are many routes from the guest house to the office, but my favourite one is through the Shahrara area. The first day Fahim took the route, I was delighted by the sight of giant mud ovens—tandoors—and I mean the really big ones. This is where they make the tandoors, Fahim explained. The street was lined with old buildings, many made of mud with wooden doors and windows. At the end of the street, the snow-capped mountains in the distance made for a perfect sighting.

Old men and children hung out in front of their homes. Younger men were busy with the tandoors, further down the road, women in blue burqas walked down the street. School children were on their way to school, skipping, without a care in the world. I loved the street, with the giant tandoors, they add a certain out of the world feel to the street and I had

The tandoor makers in Shahrara

trouble imagining how these tandoors could be transported around, leave alone how they are being used.

At the end of the Shahrara area was a beautiful monument called the Burje Shahrara, an imposing brick structure which was originally a part of the Habibia School, founded in 1904. Today, the building is part of the national security premises, and every day when we drove by, all I saw were armed guards and vehicles. Such a shame.

Guest house life

This was a long work week, packed with meetings and interviews for my project during the day. In the evenings, I had dinner in the guest house lounge. Two guests have arrived, both working on Afghanistan's constitution and law. There are new discussions and new things to learn every day.

This week, there is the distinct hum of diesel-fuelled generators as power is in short supply. Javed jan says it is because people are foolishly using room heaters when they could use bokharis. He has installed a dish on the TV in my room so that I can get more channels. Of the 400 channels I get now, most are in Arabic. I try to tune into the English language Al Jazeera, but the reception is weak. There are several French and Italian channels, should I choose to improve my language skills, but in Afghanistan, there are more interesting things to do.

Javed jan is always innovating with new projects for the guest house. Currently, he is investigating about installing a solar system. There are many discussions about this new development. I am his chief adviser, with my one claim to fame being the solar water heater in our home in Delhi. There are numerous discussions about his consultations with local Afghan traders regarding photovoltaic cells and different kinds of glass panels. Once the sun goes down, we sit around the bokhari and consider the options we have.

Almost every day, we hear about attacks in Kabul. Yesterday there were two. The first one occurred at 7:00 p.m. as we were having dinner, not too far from the guest house in the Shar-e-naw area. We could hear the sound from the blast and later, through Javed jan's sources, found out that it was a bomb blast at General Dostum's (a warlord and now Jawed Ghani's second-in-command) house. The second blast was at an NGO guest house in the area. Fortunately, no one was killed.

I had a sleepless and uneasy night after hearing about the blasts, but in the morning when the sun came up and as we gathered in the lounge for breakfast, my fears melted away. I made an omelette for everyone with tomatoes, onions, green peppers, and fresh coriander. There was whole wheat naan heated on the bokhari, cheese, cut tomatoes and cucumbers, honey and fresh persimmons. I made coffee and we sat around for a while talking in German, Dari, Urdu, and English.

Today, being Friday, the cook is on leave. Najiba jan and I will make lasagne and chocolate cake. Javed jan's snooker friends will come over for their fixed date every Friday evening. Ah, the richness of life in Kabul!

The guest house is now full. From being the only guest two weeks ago, there are now close to a dozen people here. On the first floor, there are three women lawyers associated with a German foundation's legal education project. On the ground floor, there are four Afghan lawyers, also PhD students from the provinces who are here for a workshop. They are affiliated with the German foundation's project on restorative justice. Two nights ago, French and German guests arrived and yesterday, an Indian and a Nepali, who work with the Aga Khan Foundation in Badakhshan province, checked-in.

When I am not working

I have been here for three weekends now. Friday is slower than Saturday, as till 1:00 p.m. most shops are closed for Jumma. Government offices are closed on Thursday and Friday.

On my second and third weekends, I met with friends in open air cafes. On Friday, Bele and I went for lunch and the café had a somewhat forlorn look. Bele is based at the AWN and is doing a PhD on the Afghan women's movement. We learn from each other, sharing contacts and ideas. She sits-in on some interviews for my project. At the café, only five tables are occupied, of which one has expats. Till a few years ago, this place was bustling with laughter, voices in many languages, and good cheer. There were shops with kilims, silverware, local pottery, and books. Now, most of the shops are closed and the menu is sparse. The glass case that held the pastries and other baked goods of the day, is now filled with soft drink cans.

On Chicken Street, Najiba, Bele and I visit Wahid who owns the Herat Carpet Centre. Many of his kilims grace my home and those of my family and friends. Chicken Street has changed a great deal over the years. The lovely old shops have given way to concrete buildings with communal shops, like a mini departmental complex. Business is slow as expats have been forbidden from going to the Chicken Street, a potential target for attacks.

But Wahid jan and his fellow kilim sellers have worked out a way to do business. They take their wares to the embassies directly. Business is good, says Wahid with a smile. And, as always, the visit starts with Wahid jan offering tea and disappearing into the adjoining pantry. I hear him crushing the cardamom seeds, and within minutes, there is a steaming pot of green tea with saffron and cardamom seeds and many goodies.

Back in the guest house, we have tea and the sweets that Najiba bought from the sweet shop. A cake, a white fudge-like sweet with crushed almonds, walnuts, and biscuits. After a brief rest, Najiba and I start a lasagne of broccoli, yellow and red peppers, and spinach. We send someone out for yogurt as we are not making a traditional white sauce—this one is with

Tea with Wahid jan

cheese, eggs and yogurt. The mozzarella cheese was put in the freezer by the cook so it is a mess to grate it. I decide to use a knife and hack at it.

Javed's snooker friends are here and we eat at around 7.30 p.m. Then, Tom and Fritz—who are with the German foundation—and I chat around the bokhari. Tom is part German and part British, and came to Kabul in 2011 under a Caritas project. He is married to an Indonesian and lived in Afghanistan for two years. Now he is back in Germany and working with Fritz, who heads the foundation.

Last Friday, I sat at my desk transcribing my interviews. Through the windows, I see the trees with their leaves almost all gone. It is now easy to see the birds. I love the way the sun creeps across the sky and I can see it from the room, all day.

Tea-set from Tajikistan

It was a no-power day so the genset has been on and off, as has the Internet.

Fritz needs to make a two-day trip to Tajikistan. I shamelessly ask him if he could try and buy a tea-pot for me like the ones I saw in some of the shops in Kabul, and showed him a photograph of one. I will try, he promises. Two days later, he is back and hands me two boxes—tea-pot sets and three tea cups each for the pots. I am delighted, and we sit around and drink tea in my prized cups that evening. A few days later, I do a water colour of the set. Here is a black and white version of the water colour.

In the evening, Najiba, Elisa and I make pasta with

mushroom sauce. I also bought pasta, imported from Italy, at a reasonable price. No parmesan cheese, though. Najiba made a salad and I started a soup for tonight's dinner, for Javed Jan's snooker friends and us—Elisa, Gonoosh and Hungama. Goonosh and Hungama are originally from Iran, but now live in Italy and the US respectively. Elisa is of mixed parentage and grew up in France.

My birthday was very nice with greetings from many parts of the world. A lot of love and sweets all day and, to crown it all, I was greeted with a handmade cake by Javed jan at the guest house. The Afghan lawyers gave me a set of earrings and a pendant.

It is getting colder every day. The sun is still strong and the sky is blue. At nights, with no street lights, the light from the stars brighten up the streets.

One thing that makes me believe that Afghanistan is changing is talking to young people. One young woman tells me that she is engaged. "I am 23," she says, as she shows me her ring "but will wait for a year or two to marry." "It is not a love marriage, so I want to get to know him first." Yusuf, a young man, is engaged and getting married. Love, he tells me. Thirty-five year old Humaira has a relationship with a man she has known since high school. He is a close friend and she would like to marry him and have a child. He works at a UN agency and is posted outside Afghanistan. "He wants me to shift there," she says, "but my life is here."

My friend Omar and I walked back from a café two nights ago. It was dark and the absence of street lights meant we could see the stars. He began to tell me of his friend who migrated to Canada. He misses the stars, says Omar. There are too many lights in Canada, his friend says. It is a good thing we are in

Afghanistan, I say. We both laugh, content with our lives, and the fact that we are in places where we can see stars.

Seeking health and education

At the AWN, and in Afghanistan in general, there is always talk of the lack of healthcare facilities. Afghans complain of wrong diagnoses, unnecessary surgeries and complications. Many seek help outside Afghanistan, in India, Pakistan, and Turkey.

I have seen and met many Afghans in Delhi hospitals and often referred Afghan friends to doctors I know. In 2014, Afghan medical tourism—patients and their travelling family and friends, currently estimated at 230,000 by the PHD Chamber of Commerce and Industry—is worth some $3 billion to the Indian economy. Such is the demand that the Apollo Hospital in Delhi has translators on staff, a website in Dari, and even a separate payment desk for Afghans, while the Max Hospitals in Delhi counted 6,000 Afghan patients in the last year, alone.[26]

In Delhi, most Afghans head to Lajpat Nagar, an area now known as 'Afghan Nagar' due to its high concentration of Afghans. There are two Afghan bakeries and several restaurants, many guest houses and apartments housing Afghan students, guests, medical refugees, and asylum seekers.

On the last day of November, the morning sun was slow in appearing, but when it came out, it lit up the already yellow leaves, giving them a wonderful golden glow. I go to Maryam's house for dinner and meet a Norwegian woman, working at an NGO, seeking shelter with her. That afternoon there was a blast at an NGO near her home in Karte-she; she had been on Skype with her sister in Norway and was a little tearful.

We talked about many things, including what it takes to live in a conflict-ridden country, our families, and how we think about personal security.

The doorbell rings and Maryam goes down five flights of stairs to bring the dinner that has been prepared by women in a shelter. Maryam's husband Abdul joins us after his class at the university. Abdul did a management course in India. I meet many Afghans who have studied in India. The low cost of living, scholarships, familiarity with the country's culture and language, good relations between governments, easy-to-obtain visas, and the use of English in the classroom are some of the reasons Afghans like to study in India, especially for those who cannot afford to go to Europe and the United States to study. The largest concentration of Afghan students is in Pune, Maharashtra. Some Afghans choose Uzbekistan, Tajikistan, and Turkey.

Pakistan and Iran were once top destinations, but that is no longer the case. Visa rules for Iran have become stringent in recent years, while Pakistan has become unpopular among students and the state. Many say people with Pakistani degrees do not find jobs as easily as those with degrees from India. India is a cheap and quality option.

Each year, the Indian Council for Cultural Relations (ICCR) offers 2,325 scholarships to international students. About 35 per cent of these are reserved for Afghans, the largest of any nationality. The ICCR believes the increase in the number of scholarships for Afghanistan is part of India's partnership with it. Many young women I meet in Kabul have also studied in India. They tell me that it was the best time in their lives, they felt free and loved being there. Many say it is their second home.

Winding down

Yesterday, I made a presentation of my strategic plan at the Kabul Star hotel, today is Friday and I sit at my desk, transcribing recordings. The trees are bare now. No power, and the generator has been going on and off, as has the Internet.

Tom left for Germany this morning and Fritz left at noon for Tajikistan. I offer to take John, who is based at the Australian National University and working with the foundation project, shopping. I am a terrible shopper, he says apologetically. Do not worry, I say, I'm not. He is afraid he is taking my time and offers to buy me lunch. We eat at the café around the corner and I tell him about what the women's organisations in Afghanistan are doing, especially at the grassroots level.

John is a criminologist, interested in the role of restorative justice, shame management and reintegration in crime prevention. With his colleague, Dr. Ali Wardak, a criminologist at the University of South Wales, UK, they have co-authored many papers, including Crime and War in Afghanistan, looking at the overall context and causes of the war and how it could be brought to a peaceful end. The paper includes field data from five different Afghan provinces.

An important conclusion of their work is that a peaceful end to the war in Afghanistan can only be realised if it comes from the 'bottom-up', i.e. at a grassroots level, rather than being imposed 'top-down'. However, these two sections of society must work together—and this includes engaging constructively with insurgents—in order for a ceasefire to become a reality. John and his colleagues are concerned that women have been left out of the restorative justice processes, and are looking at ways to bring them in.

Shopping was delightful, and John who was only shopping for cushion covers (as Christmas gifts) ended up with several kilims as well. Whenever he hesitated, I nudged him: support the Afghan economy, I said! Several hours later, as we walked back to the guest house laden with kilims, cushion covers, and other Christmas gift possibilities, John admitted he had had a good time. "Gosh," he said, "I never knew shopping could be so much fun!"

Wasim and I had been trying to meet. He came over and we picked up his cousin who worked at a beauty parlour. While we waited for her to come out, Wasim told me her story. She is 26, had three children and the oldest is eight. She used to live in Mazar with her husband and children until he kicked her out, and took custody of the children. Wasim says he went to Mazar, spent two days with the husband and got him to agree to let her have the children for two weeks a year, and to talk to the children on the phone.

An extra ten days

By an oversight, I stayed on in Kabul for ten extra days. I had a one-month visa and carelessly thought I could fly back one day after the expiry date. At the airport, after checking in, the officer at the immigration counter said that my visa had expired and I could not leave the country. My pleas fell on deaf ears. The officer asked me to leave the airport and re-apply for a valid visa to depart from the country. I had to go back to the guest house. Fortunately, it and my room in it were still there!

It was a circular route to get another visa to leave the country. The AWN, who had applied for my visa, had to do the paper work, going through the same channels as it had the first time around. That meant two ministries, and an AWN staffer who had to carry the application through.

Friends and those in the know said it could take from a week to ten days. I had a workshop in India which I had to cancel, my medications were running out, I was in a bit of a panic. But, at some point, I decided if I had to be in Kabul for a week, so be it. I settled down and started working, transcribing recordings and working on the project report. I read, did water colouring, wrote, and had long chats with Javed jan by the bokhari.

The Indian ambassador offered assistance and I gratefully accepted. Eventually, I was told to report to the passport office on December 24 at 7:00 a.m. When the AWN staffer and I got to the passport office at 8:00 a.m., there was already a long line of people there. It was an orderly and well organised space, about five kilometres from the guest house. We got through to the senior officers, I signed some papers in their presence and then was ushered into a waiting area. After two hours, passport in hand, I said goodbye to the young man who I had been chatting with. As we shook hands, he swung around his computer screen and said, "Look, another Indian, overstayed 400 days." "Really!" I exclaimed. "But, we will not charge him," he said. The fee was US $10 a day.

Back at the guest house, I got online with great difficulty and booked ticket. Imagine my despair when I got to the check-in counter the next day and found that I wasn't on the flight. There was some error in my online booking. After hanging around trying to figure out what to do, I managed to get through to the airline on the phone for the next day's flight to Delhi, but I had to get the ticket within the next 45 minutes as there were only two seats left and I had to pay in cash! I jumped into a taxi, got to an ATM, and then went to the city office of the airline. Triumphant, I returned to the guest house, once again.

On December 26, I finally managed to get on the flight to Delhi. Phew.

2015

"After three decades of war, people were very poor. The cities were all destroyed. There were no social facilities, no hospitals, no telecommunications, no power, no transport or agriculture. But now we have hospitals, even in very remote areas of the country.

"There are new roads, traffic lights, cars, buildings, new shopping malls, and road lights powered by solar panels. There has been a revolution of development in the country."

– Jawad Jalali, photographer

2015: The decade of transformation

Back in India, people often ask me: "Is it normal there? Is it safe?" I smile and think about the meaning of these words. What is normal or safe in Afghanistan? I tell people that Afghanistan has had three decades of war and occupation; there is insurgency and violence, but that I feel safe there.

I also tell them what Javed jan told me: I am privileged, have a car to pick me up and drop me off if I want and need to go somewhere; I stay in a safe guest house where water and electricity are ensured most of the time and someone cooks my meals. I am based in a country close by and if things get really bad, I can fly out. But many in Afghanistan may not have this life or the means to leave.

In February, the United Nations Assistance Mission in Afghanistan (UNAMA) released its 2014 annual report on Protection of Civilians in Armed Conflict in coordination with the Office of the United Nations High Commissioner for Human Rights. It said that increased ground engagement between parties in armed conflict is behind the 22 per cent rise in conflict-related deaths and injuries among Afghan civilians in 2014. Civilian casualties have also increased dramatically; the UNAMA documented 10,548 casualties in 2014, the highest number of civilian deaths and injuries recorded in a single year since 2009. This included 3,699 deaths (up by 25 per cent) and 6,849 injuries (up 21 per cent). Since 2009, the armed conflict in Afghanistan has caused 47,745 civilian casualties with 17,774 Afghans killed and 29,971 injured.[27]

For the first time since 2009, more Afghan civilians were killed and injured in ground engagements than by improvised explosive devices (IEDs) or any other tactic. The report found that civilian deaths and injuries from ground operations surged by 54 per cent, making them the leading cause of civilian casualties, and the biggest killers of Afghan women and children in 2014. Parties to the conflict increasingly used explosive weapons systems such as mortars, rockets, and grenades, sometimes indiscriminately, in civilian-populated areas with devastating consequences. The indiscriminate use of IEDs and increased number of suicide attacks by anti-government elements, added to rising civilian casualties in 2014.

According to Martine van Bijlert of the Afghan Analysts Network, in the backdrop of these casualties, Afghanistan stands at the beginning of what has hopefully been termed the Decade of Transformation. The challenges are huge: it cannot pay its army, police, and civil services; the inflated economy is deflating and the effects are being felt widely.

Large parts of the population have been living under, or just above, the poverty line, and many of them will face personal disasters—floods, drought, crop failure, unemployment, illness, crime, violence—that they will find it hard to recover from. President Ghani believes the nation's determination and resilience will pull it through; and it is true that most outside analysis tends to disregard the tenacity and potential of Afghanistan's people, focusing mainly on the country's fragility. But the odds are formidable.

Analysis is often linked to two questions: Did we fail or did we succeed? Is the situation better or worse? Will the country now fall apart or will there be progress? Our brains seem wired to demand it. But Afghanistan's reality tends to be more mixed, and the future usually holds surprises that we cannot predict.

The challenges Afghanistan faces at the beginning of 2015 are similar to those it faced in 2014, but they are not exactly the same. The constellation has changed. There is a residue from the latest turmoil—from the elections, the upsurge of attacks, the change in government—that has resulted in a combination of determination and fragility, confidence and concern, hope and fear in equal measure. The year that has just passed was another of the many 'make or break' years Afghanistan has faced. It did not break the country, but it also did not put it securely on the path to stability. Looking ahead—and if all goes well—there will probably be many more years of very precarious muddling through.

Analysts believe that amid the chaos and fragility of the national-unity government, one thing that gives Afghans hope is that both leaders speak directly about the nation's challenges. Both Ghani and Abdullah exhibit a greater interest in the economy than Karzai ever did. And while they appear to be moving forward with peace talks with the Taliban, both also seem more committed than Karzai to the military struggle against the insurgency. Much to the dismay of some of their supporters who expected positions in the new government, Ghani and Abdullah have also shown willingness to appoint officials based, at least in part, on merit. So far, the two appear unfazed by the political costs of confronting patronage and corruption.

February in Kabul

I arrived in Kabul to mild temperatures. I was carrying a woollen coat this time, unlike my trip three months ago. There had not been any snow either, which was quite unusual.

A few days later, the weather changed. There was rain, hail, and then snow. Not the sticky kind of snow, but it covered the surrounding mountains and created some slush in the streets of Kabul. For one night, Kabul turned into a winter wonderland.

North of Kabul, in Panjshir, snowfall was severe and there

were avalanches. Hundreds of people lost their lives, with homes and schools destroyed in what is being called the worst snow in three decades. Sakhi, the young man who works at the guest house, told us that one of his close relatives had died in the avalanche.

Power lines from Tajikistan and Uzbekistan to Kabul were knocked out and the city was in the dark for 48 hours. Officials said that repairing all the cables would take a month. Javed jan's experiments with the infrastructure finally paid off. Since the last time I was here, he had installed a solar energy system; between this, the genset and the bokharis, we had enough to keep us warm.

My assignment involves talking to young men and women about their work and life. Almost every one of them has been a refugee in Pakistan or Iran. Since their return, they have been to college, got degrees, and are working in various jobs. They have some reservations about the future, are concerned about security, and really do not want the Taliban to come back.

While the president and CEO of Afghanistan strive to handle matters of state, some insurgency in the capital continues, and more frequently in the provinces.

The Afghans are worried about the Islamic State (IS), called Daesh here, infiltrating their country, and feel that this is a new and unnecessary threat in an already conflicted society. On the other hand, it is heartening to hear of efforts being made to study Sharia law and use it to tackle prejudice and violence of all kinds. Javed jan tells me there are serious attempts by the government to stamp out the Taliban in the provinces, but helicopters would be most helpful, a challenge for an already impoverished and indebted government.

I am in Kabul to assist an NGO to prepare a three-year strategy; their research focuses on issues of women, peace and security. As a part of my assignment, I become aware of case studies of women at the grassroots level involved in the peace process. The studies highlight that most disputes in provinces take place within or between families. Forced marriage is the most common source of family strife, but domestic violence also figures prominently. Societies living with conflict and a high degree of militarisation typically witness higher levels of gender-based violence as a function of many factors—people have been brutalised by their experiences, weapons are easily available, and young people have learnt that violence is acceptable behaviour.

What are the disputes that women peacemakers face? One involved squatters in a cemetery shared by seven villages; another was the lack of housing for a community of nomads, where the peacemaker arranged housing and also organised a school running out of a local mosque; a third was a dispute between two people—living upstream and downstream—over trees that choked the flooding. These issues require legal and technical solutions. The peacemakers listen and identify the appropriate solutions, not letting their lack of formal training or experience deter them or impede their work.

Involving the community is essential for peacemakers. People come to the 'learning circles' and engage with new ideas. What are learning circles? In seventh century, when Afghanistan became part of the Islamic world, there was a surge in the number and kinds of educational institutions. The most prominent were mosque schools, maktabs or learning circles which were housed in mosques. They were open to the public and led by scholars who specialised in subjects from the Quran to poetry and discussions on literature.

Currently, there are circles for those who may never have studied formally or travelled widely but have deep knowledge of the religious canon. The circles identify and encourage people to confidently engage the Taliban on religious questions. Many of these circles are constituted formally or informally by women with shared interests—cultural or literary, or common experience of some capacity building and training.

Some peacemakers were involved in processes that resulted in over one thousand insurgents laying down arms and entering the peace process. This required sustained interaction with the families, either in a routine setting or including them proactively in public forums.

These women show incredible courage. One peacemaker has survived seven suicide attacks, but this has only reinforced her determination to carry on. They are persistent and tenacious, they are the peacemakers of Afghanistan.

On February 26, a young Afghan woman artist, Kubra Khademi, posted on Facebook that she would be on the streets at 3:00 p.m. sharp for her street performance called "Armour". Khademi's inspiration for the performance came from several traumatising experiences of being touched or grabbed by men while walking down the street. The first incident occurred when she was four or five years old, living as a refugee with her parents in Iran during the Soviet war in Afghanistan. She was so ashamed after the incident that she didn't tell her family. Instead, she hid in the bathroom where she cried and shook with fear while imagining having some kind of underwear that could scare off such pursuers. Kubra was touched again when she returned to Kabul in 2008. This time she screamed in the street and when people gathered, instead of helping her, they criticised her for making such a fuss over the incident. No one said anything to the man who had assaulted her. For her street art performance, Khademi designed and wore an exaggerated breast and buttock armour in a crowded street of Kabul.

Men and women reacted predominantly negatively, both in person and on social media. Khademi was mocked, condemned, called a whore, and threatened. Her protest was seen as offensive to women and to Afghanistan, and as a stunt to promote western culture. Her outfit was sexualised and viewed as something she donned only to draw attention to her body parts. Not surprisingly, Khademi and a few of the women accompanying her, were touched and groped by male spectators.

Postscript

It is May 2015, and as I finish writing, President Ghani has just left Delhi. Media coverage has been about his efforts to contain the insurgency and cross-border terrorism between Pakistan and Afghanistan. India has promised cooperation and trade, and delivered three long overdue planes.

In Kabul, there are continued and regular protests on violence against women, with several men coming out in support of the cause. On March 8th, a day after I left Kabul and in celebration of International Women's Day, a group of Afghan men wearing burqas gathered outside the Afghan Independent Human Rights Commission to protest violence against women.

A week after I left Kabul, a 28 year old Afghan woman called Farkhunda was lynched in Kabul for 'speaking out'. According to BBC reports, Farkhunda, an Islamic scholar, had been arguing with a mullah about his practice of selling charms to women at a shrine. In the course of the argument, she was accused of burning the Quran, and a crowd that gathered beat her to death. According to eye witnesses, she was hit with bats, stamped on, driven over, and her body dragged by a car before being set on fire and dumped into the dried-up Kabul river. The attack, near the Shah-du-Shamshaira mosque and shrine, is thought to have been the first of its kind in Afghanistan.[28]

Hundreds of Afghans came out on the streets to protest the attack. The event raised new questions about the pace of reform in Afghanistan. The government acknowledged it was a serious and heinous act. Police detained 18 people and 13 policemen were suspended for having failed to do enough to stop the attack.

According to *Al Jazeera*, Farkhunda's murder reveals a nation that has changed. Her last agonising and brutal hours were captured on mobile phone cameras by witnesses and those in the mob who attacked her. Videos of the assault circulated widely on social media. The incident sparked nationwide outrage and soul-searching, as well as a civil society movement seeking to limit the power of clerics, strengthen the rule of law, and improve women's rights.

Breaking with tradition, women's rights activists carried the coffin at Farkhunda's funeral, a role usually performed by men.

After decades of being kept at home and discouraged from having a public life, women are claiming this life for themselves. Young teenage girls are taking to sports in an unbelievable way. Afghanistan has a national women's football team and there are around 25 such teams around the country. On February 16, 2012, the team scored a 2–0 win against Qatar, their first official international victory. A women cyclists' team trains three times a week on unused roads, on a plain north of Kabul and in the province of Bamiyan.

Then there is boxing. If it is unusual to see a woman representing Afghanistan at the Olympic games, her choice of sport is even more surprising. Sadaf Rahimi, the only female member of the national team, and only the third female Olympic athlete to represent the country, is a boxer. Now 18, her early childhood was a time when women were banned from sports under the Taliban. She now trains at the Ghazi stadium in Kabul, where the old regime staged public executions, with many of the condemned being women.

Sohaila Abdullah, writing in the Indian business paper, *Mint Lounge*, describes young teenage girls who are part of the global Skateistan project, which provides physical and psychic space for children to develop strength, trust and confidence. In Kabul, girls who earlier sold tea and gum are now expert skateboarders. They collect at the Zarnegar Park in Kabul and "live out their dreams while they do heel flips, nollies, 360s and nose slides", writes Abdullah, creating their own moments of joy.

The Afghan army and police are continuing to fight insurgency while maintaining law and order. According to National Public Radio, while smaller operations are being conducted as part of Operation Rescue, a larger Afghan effort of large-scale combat operations are being planned, organised and fought by Afghan forces. Afghans are now in charge of fighting the Taliban—with no Americans in sight—and comparatively speaking, they are doing rather well. They are relatively well-equipped, organised and led. They look like a professional army and are eager to go out and take on the Taliban. It is a far cry from just a few years ago, when Americans were in the lead. Then, for instance, American soldiers would turn up for dawn patrols in full combat gear, ready to go—and the Afghans would be sleepy, half-dressed, and sometimes smelling of hashish. Now, exclusively Afghan troops, joined this day by local police, are fanning out into a village that is the site of some suspicious targets.

Talks with the Taliban continue under the Ghani government. The Afghan and Pakistani governments are battling intertwined insurgencies. Using this mutual interest, they have tried to improve relations, and Pakistan has become a mediator in the peace process in Afghanistan. Nonetheless, the recent revelation of Taliban leader Mullah Mohammad Omar's 2013 death accentuated a leadership struggle within the movement; and the new leader of the Taliban, Mullah Akhtar Mansoor, does not enjoy full support either. Moreover, Taliban, as any non-monolithic organisation, was divided on the topic of holding any meaningful talks from the very beginning.[29]

The talks continue, as do the attacks, evidence of the Taliban's disunity, but this has not made the group any less lethal. It shows that the Afghan government cannot effectively oppose the Taliban. These attacks are also evidence of the fact that a part of the Taliban leadership does not support the peace process between the Afghan government and the militants.

In 2014, the Pakistani government started a military operation Operation Zarb-e-Azb in North Waziristan and Khyber, along the Pakistan-Afghanistan border, as a renewed effort against militancy. The Pakistani military put pressure on the various militant groups, including the Tehrik-i-Taliban Pakistan (TTP), the Islamic Movement of Uzbekistan, the East Turkestan Islamic Movement, Lashkar-e-Jhangvi, Al-Qaeda, Jundallah and the Haqqani network.

Within Afghanistan, questions are raised about the claims of representation. Heather Barr of Human Rights Watch reports that when an Afghan government delegation met Taliban representatives for talks in Qatar in the second week of May, several unusual things happened. It was the first time that three women were included in a 20 member Afghan government delegation. The women who attended said they found the Taliban delegation surprisingly ready to discuss issues with them. The Afghan government and its key partners, including the US, have largely failed to include women in previous talks with the Taliban. This meeting was the first such discussion after President Ashraf Ghani took office in September 2014.[30]

When activists have pushed for women's participation in talks with the Taliban, one response from donors and the Afghan government, behind closed doors, has been that this demand is counter-productive because the Taliban would refuse to negotiate with women. The May meeting should end that argument for good. Ghani's inclusion of women in these talks is a positive step and should set the vital precedent that no future talks will go forward without women in significant roles.

A second unusual development was that the Taliban said some positive things about women's rights. Taliban participants reportedly pledged support for women's education up to the university level and vowed to permit women to work outside the home, "even in male-dominated professions like engineering." Taliban negotiators also expressed support for women's participation in politics, women's right to inherit, and to choose a husband. Some of these positions even appear in the Taliban's written statement about the meeting.

What to make of this? One should hope very much that this is all true, but Afghan women who have lived through years of the Taliban rule and the anti-women attacks in the years since, have every reason to be sceptical.

As I stay abreast of the news in Afghanistan, my mind goes back to my first visit in 2004. The Afghanistan of today is very different. While some things are the same, many things have changed for the better.

On a typical day in Kabul, the sun rises and sets, children go to school, men and women go to work. The open markets are laden with fruits and vegetables, the kebab and naan wallahs do brisk business, and the streets are full of people on bicycles, buses and cars. The old and the new, rich and poor, literate and illiterate, come together. Afghans travel within and out of Afghanistan and people from all over come to Afghanistan. There is music, poetry, laughter and love. There is violence, sadness and uncertainty. There is despair, but there is also hope.

All in the space of a day, in Kabul.

Notes

[1] United Nations (E/CN.6/2002/5), 2002, The Situation of Women in Afghanistan, http://www.un.org/events/women/2002/sit.htm. Accessed on November 10, 2014.

[2] The Constitution of Afghanistan, www.afghanembassy.com. Accessed on August 22, 2015.

[3] Agence France Press, 2012, http://tribune.com.pk/story/336804/afghan-women-tv-presenters-told-more-veil-less-make-up/. Accessed on September 8, 2015.

[4] International Media Support, 2013 Afghanistan: Female Journalists Battle Threats and Discrimination, www.mediasupport.org. Accessed on September 8, 2015.

[5] Thomas Wide, "Istalif Pottery", *Steppe* 2011, Issue 5.

[6] William Dalrymple, *Return of a King: The Battle for Afghanistan* (London: Bloomsbury, 2012).

[7] See www.afghankitchenrecipes.com/. Accessed on January 2015.

[8] United Nations Office on Drugs and Crime and the Islamic Republic of Afghanistan, Ministry of Counter Narcotics, *Afghanistan Opium Survey 2012: Summary Findings.*

[9] M. Siddieq Noorzoy, *Afghanistan's Children: The Tragic Victims of 30 Years of War*, Middle East Institute 2012, http://www.mei.edu/content/afghanistans-children-tragic-victims-30-years-war. Accessed in April 2015.

[10] Library of Congress Federal Research Division, **2006**, *Afghanistan Country Profile.*

[11] Andrew Reynolds and John Carey, 2012, *Fixing Afghanistan's Electoral System: Arguments and Options for Reform.* Briefing Paper Series, Afghanistan Research and Evaluation Unit.

[12] Anna Badkhen, "Afghanistan: Can an Entire Country Have PTSD?", Pulitzer Center on Crisis Reporting 2012, http://pulitzercenter.org/reporting/afghanistan-post-traumatic-stress-disorder-mental-health-care-genocide-violence. Accessed on April 10, 2015.

[13] Barbara Lopez Cardozo, Oleg O Bilukha, et al, "Mental health, social functioning, and disability in postwar Afghanistan", *The Journal of the American Medical Association* 2004, 292(5):575-84.

[14] Anna Badkhen, "Afghanistan: Can an Entire Country Have PTSD?", op. cit.

[15] Internews and Altai Consulting 2012, Signposting Success: Civil Society in Afghanistan, https://www.internews.org/sites/default/files/resources/AltaiConsulting-Signposting_Success_FinalReport.pdf. Accessed on March 10, 2015.

[16] Asia Foundation, *Survey of the Afghan People, 2009.*

[17] Martine van Bijlert, 2009, "How to Win an Afghan Election—Perceptions and Practices", Afghanistan Analysts Network.

[18] Shahrazad Akbar and Zubaida Akbar, 2011, "Elections and Conflict in Afghanistan", Friedrich Ebert Stiftung: International Policy Analysis, http://library.fes.de/pdf-files/iez/08587.pdf. Accessed on April 7, 2015.

[19] *Wall Street Journal*, 2010, "Karzai Divides Afghanistan in Reaching out to Taliban", www.wsj.com/.../SB10001424052748703720004575476913015061570.

[20] Åsne Seierstad, *The Bookseller of Kabul* (New York: Back Bay Books, 2002).

[21] Joel Brinkley, 2013, "Young Afghans suffer mental illness", Politico. http://www.politico.com/story/2013/06/many-young-afghans-suffering-mental-illness-with-nonstop-war-092533#ixzz3lRsWIS1q. Accessed on April 10, 2015.

[22] Ibid.

[23] Internews and Altai Consulting 2012, "Signposting Success: Civil Society" op. cit.

[24] Martine van Bijlert, "Fear, Hope and Determination: Afghanistan and the 2014 Syndrome", Afghan Analysts Network.

[25] Mujib Mashal, "Afghanistan's Team of Rivals: Can two former political foes overcome a bitter election stalemate to combat the country's endemic corruption?" *Al Jazeera America*, 2015.

[26] Medical Tourism Magazine, 2014, "Afghanistan Medical Tourism Patients find Welcome Mats in India."

[27] UNAMA and UNHCR, 2014, Annual Report on Protection of Civilians in Armed Conflict.

[28] BBC, 2015, "Afghan woman Farkhunda lynched in Kabul 'for speaking out".

[29] Heather Barr, *Dispatches: Too Early to Cheer Taliban Support for Women's Rights*. Human Rights Watch, May 2015

[30] Southfront, 2015, Afghanistan map of war 2015: Taliban's disunity hasn't made the group any less lethal, http://southfront.org/afghanistan-map-of-war-august-16-2015/, Accessed on May 4, 2015.

References

Carol Faubert, Mary Kaldo, Saeed Niazi, Rajeev Pillay, 2006, "Case Study Afghanistan. Human Security: Evaluation of UNDP Assistance to Conflict Affected Areas", UNDP Evaluation Office.

National Democratic Institute for International Affairs, USAID, 2006, *The September 2005 Parliamentary and Provincial Council Elections in Afghanistan.*

International Crisis Group, Asia Briefing No. 31, 30 March 2004, *Elections and Security in Afghanistan.*

Indira A.R. Lakshmanan and Eltaf Najafizada, January 4, 2012, "Taliban Takes First Step Toward Talks to End Decade-Long Afghanistan War." *Bloomberg Business*, January 4, 2012.

Michael Semple, Theo Farrell, Anatol Lieven, Rudra Chaudhuri, 2012, "Taliban Perspectives on Reconciliation", Royal United Services Institute.

Robert Hossal, 2012, http://www.smartwar.org/2012/01/talking-with-the-taliban-a-timeline/. Accessed on March 6, 2015

See www.afghancooking.net/afghan.../afghan-new-year-dried-fruit-medley, posted March 20, 2012. Accessed on May 22, 2013.

Martine van Bijlert, 2015, *After the Rollercoaster Comes What? Afghanistan in 2015,* Afghan Analysts Network.

Human Rights, United Nations Assistance Mission in Afghanistan, Kabul and Office of the United Nations High Commissioner for Human Rights, Geneva, 8 July 2009, *Silence is Violence: End the Abuse of Women in Afghanistan.*

Jennifer Heath and Jawed Zahedied, *Children of Afghanistan: The Path to Peace* (Austin: University of Texas Press, 2014).

Women, Peace and Security Research Institute, Afghanistan, 2015, *Peacemakers' Tales from Afghanistan.*

National Public Radio, May 7, 2015, "Afghan Army Makes Progress; Will Government Services Follow?"

Al Jazeera and Associated Press, 6 May 2015, Four sentenced to death over brutal Afghan mob killing.

Sohaila Abdullah, May 2, 2015, "I Won't Stop: Girls on Wheels", *Mint Lounge.*

Acknowledgements

In the winter of 2006, over lunch at a mutual friend's house in south Delhi, I mentioned to friend and publisher, Ritu Menon, that I was leaving for Kabul soon. Keep a diary, she said.

I didn't quite keep a diary, but I did start a blog called *Letter from Afghanistan* one month after I got to Kabul. So, a major thank you to Ritu, for planting the thought and eventually, helping to put the book together.

There would be no blogs or a book without the generosity of the people and organisations that invited me to Afghanistan to work with them. Through their work, I was able to experience Afghanistan the way I did.

Chandni Joshi and Sumantra Guha of UNIFEM, now UN Women, made possible my first trip to Kabul. Subsequently, Internews Europe and the training Centre Nai, Oxfam, Checchi Consulting, the Afghan Women's Network and the Research Institute for Women, Security and Peace, invited me to conduct trainings, assessments and strategic planning for their organisations in Kabul.

From 2004–2015, I met and worked with many individuals in Afghanistan who are now friends—Agathe Dalisson, Roya Aziz, Aliaxey, Mujeeb Khavatgar, Abdul Wahid Hashimi, Vic Goetz, Rachel Wareham, Tatjana Schenke, Ricardo Grassi, Rolf Paasch, Linda Libront, Mary McCabe, Wazhma Frogh, Hasina Safi, Mary Akrami, Leeda Yaqoobi, Arslan Muradi, Asila Wardak, Shinkai Karokhail, Ahmed Zia Hidary, Ahmad

Shuja Momuzai, Ashraf Shahalemi, Latifa Ramazan, Babrak Osman, Samira Hamidi and Naveed Zulfiqar. I am deeply appreciative of what they brought into my life and time in Afghanistan.

I was often accompanied by interpreters and drivers to meetings in Kabul, and during my visits to the provinces. Without their assistance I would not have been able to learn about and witness the many dimensions of the co-existing beauty and despair of Afghanistan.

The Afghans I met—in shops, markets and streets and the support staff of the organisations I was contracted by—all shared their stories, wit, and down-to-earth pragmatism, which were refreshing and heart-warming.

The NGOs, members of the media, staff of government ministries and the UN system who welcomed me and shared their dreams, hopes and heartaches in doing what they set out to do—to build a new Afghanistan.

An exceptional debt to the student trainees in my classes in 2006 at the training centre at Nai, who opened their hearts and minds and let me into their lives, talking courageously about topics close to their hearts, difficult as they were.

The journalists, analysts and fiction writers whose work gave me another perspective on Afghanistan and filled in gaps in my knowledge and experience.

Thanks to the feedback, suggestions and advice from friends Supriya Singh, Gautam Bhatia and Ashok Agarwal. For the period I was gone from home, the support and love of Mahesh Uppal, my husband, and Kabir Uppal, my son.

Finally, the country of Afghanistan which I serendipitously entered, fell in love with and is always with me, wherever I am.